VIRGIN SNOW

To Joan,
God bless you as
you continue to leave
His mark in the world.

In Christ,
Becky Jesus
matt 5:16

VIRGIN SNOW

LEAVING YOUR MARK IN THE WORLD

BECKY TOEWS

WinePressPublishing
Your Book, Defined.

WinePress Publishing (PO Box 428, Enumclaw, WA 98022) functions only as book publisher. As such, the ultimate design, content, editorial accuracy, and views expressed or implied in this work are those of the author.

Unless otherwise noted, all Scriptures are taken from the *Holy Bible, New International Version®, NIV®*. Copyright © 1973, 1978, 1984 by Biblica, Inc.™ Used by permission of Zondervan. All rights reserved worldwide. WWW. ZONDERVAN.COM

Scripture references marked KJV are taken from the *King James Version* of the Bible.

Scripture references marked NASB are taken from the *New American Standard Bible*, © 1960, 1963, 1968, 1971, 1972, 1973, 1975, 1977 by The Lockman Foundation. Used by permission.

Scripture references marked MSG are taken from *The Message Bible* © 1993 by Eugene N. Peterson, NavPress, PO Box 35001, Colorado Springs, CO 80935, 4ᵗʰ printing in USA 1994. Published in association with the literary agency—Alive Comm. PO Box 49068, Colorado Springs, CO 80949. Used by permission.

ISBN 13: 978-1-60615-036-8
ISBN 10: 1-60615-036-7
Library of Congress Catalog Card Number: 2009942284

In loving memory of Grandpa

Everyone should have a Grandpa Creech

CONTENT

"I believe in Christianity as I believe the sun has risen. Not only because I see it—but because by it I see everything else."

—C. S. Lewis

ACKNOWLEDGMENTS

I'M DEEPLY GRATEFUL to so many for the parts they have played in helping me with *Virgin Snow*. First I want to thank Marty and Lisa Creech for generously providing a *pleasant inn* where I could work... the beauty and peace of Lakeside. Thank you to Bob Hostettler whose suggestions at conception were so helpful. David Hawkes, thanks for your insightful critique, prayers and support. Dale Johnson, what a firestorm you ignited when you made the casual remark of where I should ski! I'd also like to thank all my former and present students at HATS and Lancaster Bible College for making me a better writer. Thanks, Mom, for your generous support and for picking up the slack the many times I was glued to the computer. Bethany and Josiah, your names are sprinkled throughout the book. I'm grateful for how you have allowed yourselves to live in a fishbowl. To my spiritual family at New Covenant Christian Church, your support and love over the years has meant more to me than words could say. This book would not be a reality without you. To Chip... no one has encouraged me more in this project than you. Thank you from the bottom of my heart. ...*in my life, I love you more.*

Finally, thank you, Lord Jesus for granting me this opportunity to publish my *opus*. May you be glorified through it.

INTRODUCTION
FINDING YOUR MARK

*His registration number is on you. Your DNA matters because the
essence of who you are matters and whose you are by design matters....
Consider it God's sovereign imprint on you.*

—Ravi Zacharias
The Grand Weaver

VIRGIN SNOW. FRESH tracks moving through uncharted territory
saying, "I was here"—identifiably here. Footprints in snowy fields or on
sandy beaches voice that someone has passed through, an impression
was made. Whether we cautiously inched our way across or plodded
the course with daring perseverance, the landscape is altered. Kind of
like life.

We've been given a season on this earth to go where no one else
has gone and to do what no one else has done. Each call is distinctive,
unique, personal—maybe even a bit peculiar. Every life has twists and
turns. Often we don't know where we're going, and we lose track of
where we've been. Sometimes we don't feel there's a plan or pattern for
the best or worst of our experiences. But like a skier who encounters a
hillside of virgin snow, the significance we long for crystallizes when we
make new discoveries.

Anyone who has watched *American Idol* is familiar with the point
in the program where contestants stand before the judges to hear them

critique their performance. Anxiously the singers wait, listening for words that could determine the direction of their life's careers—hoping *not* to hear Simon Cowell say, "It was forgettable." This strikes me as symbolic. Who of us wants to reach the end of life only to look back and think that it was *forgettable*? Don't we all long to know our lives have had meaning?

I believe that there's a basic human need to leave a legacy that says "my life mattered." Look around and you will see evidence of this drive everywhere. I recently saw this when I attended a writers' conference. I was impressed with the sheer number of people who attended—people who were looking for a venue to tell their story or impart a life lesson. I have observed this as I've walked down corridors and seen doors with gold plaques engraved with signatures: "In memory of…" I've noticed it as I've read the names carved in granite at Washington DC's monuments. No matter what age, it seems the need for significance surfaces, from the retired school teacher who invites me to her house to view the quilts she's meticulously crafted, to the thousand "Look, Mommy, see what I did" requests. We all want to leave a mark.

I'm not talking about marks of fame or notoriety, however. Our significance doesn't rest on whether we've won a Nobel Prize or have been voted "Teacher of the Year." Those are marks, but not necessarily the indelible ones described here. Certainly the drive to live a meaningful life is an aspect of being created in the image of God, but it would be a mistake to equate our value with observable success only. It's not the biblical model, which reminds us that "the greatest in the kingdom is the least" (Matthew 18:1–4) and "the first will be last" (Matthew 20:16).

So what do we mean when we say that we want to leave our mark? As Christians, we hope that the marks we make reflect the ones God has made on us. I believe those are the only marks that will last. Those aspects of God that we allow to be engraved in our character are the ones that will never fade. The lessons God teaches us about faith, hope, and sacrificial love are the indelible imprints that will be passed on, because they encompass eternal value.

This book is aimed at those who want to leave that kind of mark—an eternal mark. The message in these pages is for those who want to discover how to embrace the marks God desires to leave through them. These marks are formed in our everyday experiences.

Jesus' own marks were a direct result of his responding daily to what the Father told him to do. And just as God made himself known to Jesus in the "warp and woof" of life, as Francis Schaeffer often said, so Jesus reveals himself to people while they're "on the way." He met the disciples on the road to Emmaus, Saul on the road to Damascus, and Mary on her way from the tomb. He meets me while I'm sipping a caramel macchiato at Barnes and Noble, listening to Michael Card sing "Be Thou My Vision" in concert, applauding the sunset at Acadia's Cadillac Mountain, and reveling in a brisk morning walk by Lake Erie. He enters our everyday comings and goings and checks our direction. We're carried to fresh thinking that interrupts the ordinary and surprises us with the delight of discovery. These discoveries engrave the marks that inevitably shape who we are and where we're going. They help make sense out of where we've been and give us a clearer perspective on how the pieces of our lives fit together.

I love the story of the woman with the alabaster jar who poured perfume on Jesus (Mark 14:3–9). When she was criticized by others who were present, Jesus rose to her defense. "Leave her alone," said Jesus. "Why are you bothering her? She has done a beautiful thing to me." I especially like the first part of verse eight: "She did what she could."

This woman didn't hold an evangelistic revival that brought hundreds to Christ. She didn't write best-selling books. She didn't minister to the poor in Calcutta. She did what *she could*. She took the natural resource she was given—an ordinary alabaster bottle of perfume—and used it to pour out her devotion to Jesus. She could have said things like: "I don't have anything to give." "I'm a woman, and I can't barge in on this men's meeting." "People will think I'm stupid." But she wasn't distracted by any of those thoughts. She was propelled by one focus—her love for Jesus. *She did what she could,* and because of it, Jesus said that she would be remembered wherever the gospel was preached. Indeed, this dear woman left an indelible mark, one we'll explore in greater depth later on.

I don't know where you are "on the way" right now. Maybe you're trying to persevere through difficult circumstances. Maybe, as Brennan Manning describes, you're "on the far side of despair," waiting for promises to be fulfilled. Perhaps you're wrestling with issues of forgiveness or obedience, or you might just need a fresh perspective on how to hear God or how to stand resolute in an increasingly antagonistic culture. Wherever you are, you have been called to leave marks in this world that no one else can leave.

As you work through life's issues, I hope this book helps you recognize how God wants to use your unique experiences to mark you with virtues such as truth, mercy, fruitfulness, and trust. I pray that these pages will heighten your awareness of the virgin snow that is beckoning you to leave your tracks.

CHAPTER 1

RESOLVED!
THE MARK OF TRUTH

We hold these truths to be self-evident...
Declaration of Independence

A FEW YEARS ago, Christina Hoff Sommers, Philosophy professor at Clark University, published an article entitled "Teaching the Virtues," causing quite a stir in the academic community. In it she attacked educational institutions for teaching ethics solely in terms of social injustice, like the oppression of women and environmental irresponsibility. She argued ethics should also include instruction on individual decency and honesty. One of her colleagues criticized her for giving in to "middle-class morality" by thinking of ethics in traditional moral terms. But at the end of the semester, this same colleague was shocked to discover that over half of her students had plagiarized the take-home exam for their *ethics* course![1] She had taught ethics in a vacuum, disconnected from universal standards of right and wrong, and the result was a failure to integrate all areas of personal responsibility. Her shock reveals that people can't really live as if there are no moral absolutes, even when they purport there are none. It's not the way God created the world.

Just as absolute truth carries with it a mantle of personal responsibility, watered-down truth appeals to our irresponsibility. Consequently, we live under a cloud of "no-fault" insurance, "no-fault" divorce, and even "no-fault" history, where teachers are encouraged not to blame any particular group for atrocities like the Holocaust and 9/11. This lack of accountability pulls at the very threads that hold our society together, causing us, like the psalmist, to cry out, "When the foundations are being destroyed what can the righteous do?" (Psalm 11:3).

When our founding fathers signed the Declaration of Independence, they recognized that there were certain truths upon which our freedom rested. They realized that without these truths, there would be no basis for liberty. They were resolved in holding to these self-evident truths to the point of pledging their "lives," their "fortunes," and their "sacred honor."

As Christians, our freedom also stands on truth. Jesus said, "If you hold to my teaching, you are really my disciples. Then you will know the truth, and the truth will set you free" (John 8:31–32). If we lessen our resolve in holding on to truth, we will not only forfeit our freedom, but we will also leave behind a track marked with distortion, alteration, and cultural adaptation.

In every area we face, it is the resoluteness to stand firm in the truth that keeps us free and, in the end, marks us with the significance we long for. Many of the problems we encounter can at least begin to be *solved* with *resolve*:

- Your marriage has grown cold and you feel like giving up.
  Resolved: "What God has joined together, let man not separate" (Matthew 19:6).
- You're single and tempted to compromise your pledge of purity.
  Resolved: I will "flee from sexual immorality" (1 Corinthians 6:18).
- You have financial concerns and don't know how next month's bills will be paid.
  Resolved: "And my God will meet all [my] needs" (Philippians 4:19).
- You are faced with a seemingly hopeless situation.
  Resolved: "Anyone who trusts in [Christ] will never be put to shame" (Romans 10:11).

"Resolved"—what a wonderful word, a magnificent mindset for those who refuse to compromise the truth! I think of Shadrach, Meshach, and Abednego. They were exiled to Babylon at the time king Nebuchadnezzar decreed that everyone had to worship the ninety-foot statue he had erected or be thrown into a blazing furnace. These men didn't budge. They were resolute that they would never bow to another God, even if it meant they would meet a horrible death. They said, "If we are thrown into the blazing furnace, the God we serve is able to save us from it, and he will rescue us from your hand, O king. But even if he does not, we want you to know, O king, that we will not serve your gods or worship the image of gold you have set up" (Daniel 3:17–18). They would rather have been burned alive than deny God!

Their refusal made Nebuchadnezzar so furious that he ordered the furnace be heated seven times hotter than usual before he had them bound and thrown into the raging inferno. But before they hit the flames, one was with them who looked "like the son of the gods." This "one" didn't miraculously remove them from the fire, but he supernaturally shielded them from being burned. Their resolve to trust God had not been misplaced.

And neither is ours. There are many fires we may have to walk through in our life of faith. But as we resolve to be marked with truth, we will forge a path of authenticity for generations to come and enjoy the liberty that characterizes God's children. Several truths might be considered foundational, but there are three that especially lay the groundwork in a "Christian's declaration."

Truth #1: Put First Things First.

The first thing to put first is God. The primary commandment God gave to Israel was "You shall have no other gods before me" (Exodus 20:3). He even gave the reason for this command. The preceding verse says, "I am the Lord your God who brought you out of Egypt…" They were to place God above all else because of what he had done for them. He had delivered them from slavery and turned them into a massive, independent nation. Without his intervention, they would still be making bricks. He gave them the opportunity to breathe free, to own their own land, and to leave a rich heritage to their children rather than a legacy of chains. Putting him first was supposed to be an expression of their gratitude and loyalty.

In the New Testament we are told to love God with all our heart, soul, and mind (Matthew 22:37)—for the same reason. We may not have lived as slaves in Egypt, but it's only through God's sending Christ that we have life at all. Nothing is to creep in and take the place of our wholehearted devotion to him.

As human beings, we were created to be worshipers, and if we don't worship God, we will worship something or someone else. It could be another person, our family, or our profession. The desire for money, fame, or even ministry might lure us. But anything or anyone we prioritize over God or even place beside him—no matter how good or pure it may seem—will eventually corrupt us. Jesus said, "Seek first the kingdom of God and His righteousness and all these things shall be added unto you" (Matthew 6:33 KJV). When we prioritize him, as this passage indicates, everything else will fall into place. Once the right order is established, God can freely bless us because our tendency to elevate other "things" is checked.

One of "these things" that God adds to us is the capacity to develop rich relationships with other people. We have been given the opportunity to relate to others on a deep, intimate level as part of our human experience. From the beginning of creation, God recognized that it was not good for man to be alone, so he gave flesh and blood companionship to cure the loneliness (Genesis 2:18). The psalmist wrote in Psalm 133:1, "How good and pleasant when brothers live together in unity." Jesus prayed that his disciples would be one as he and the Father were one (John 17:22). The passage from Matthew gives us the means by which this happens: Seek him first. This is one of the most basic but significant truths God has ever revealed to me.

The greatest aspiration I had growing up was to get married. Fortunately, as I grew older, the perfect man was no longer confined to being the future football coach at Portsmouth West High School. Thinking back, I can't remember a time when I wasn't praying for a Christian husband. Perhaps because my parents divorced when I was young, I longed for a stable, Christian home. Although I always prayed for a Christian husband, I really didn't think God would pick someone who was *cool enough* (I confess my arrogance), so I tended to date non-Christians and then ask God to save them. That was not the right order, but God, in his grace, spared me from what could have been a disaster.

While I was in graduate school at the University of Colorado, two guy friends and I decided to hitchhike to the Grand Canyon. We spent a few days there, hiking down the craggy cliffs and taking in the rugged beauty before heading back to Boulder. We stood on the outskirts of Flagstaff all morning with our thumbs out, trying to catch a ride, but to no avail. Then a little Austin MG drove up, and before the driver could say, "I don't have room for all three of you," we were packed in. We drove into the night, and by the time we reached Albuquerque, all four of us were looking for a place to unroll our sleeping bags and crash. However, I didn't exactly "crash," and neither did Chip, the driver of the MG. Instead, he and I stayed up the whole night talking. Thinking we never would see each other again, we were exceptionally transparent in our conversation. As a result, neither of us had ever experienced the depth of communication that we did that night. When he left us the next morning to head in the opposite direction, I wondered if we would ever meet again.

About a year later, Chip and his friend, Bob, rented a small Cessna aircraft and flew to Boulder to visit me. We were both a bit surprised to find the level of communication that had sparked when we first met was still alive. By this time my walk with God had solidified, and I was clear about my faith. I told him that if there was to be anything in the future, it would only happen if God was first in both our lives. I no longer prayed, "God, save him" (so I could get what I wanted). I prayed, "God, let your will be done."

The following winter Chip came to see me again, but this time he was driving his old VW bus. He drove about 1,700 miles from Lancaster, Pennsylvania, to Boulder, and along the way his heater broke. He had driven most of the way without heat! When he showed up at my apartment, he was wearing about four layers of clothing and his beard was covered with icicles, but he was smiling ear-to-ear. I'll never forget his words: "I've been talking to a friend of yours for the last few hours."

We were married on a mountaintop that May. I can honestly say that on the morning of the wedding, even though I was hopelessly in love, I could still offer to the Lord, "If this is not what *you* want, and you have led me this far for a reason I can't see, let your will be done."

Inscribed on Chip's wedding ring was the passage from Matthew 6:33. It was the first time in my life I had prioritized God in a relationship. Not only had he answered my childhood prayers, but also he had added to me the greatest gift I could have imagined. When we put God first, he will add everything else we need. Why? Because he's our Father.

Truth #2: God Primarily Wants Us to Know Him as Father.

Many names are used for God throughout Scripture. A few include: El Shaddai, which means *God Almighty*; Jehovah-Shalom—*the Lord is peace*; Jehovah-Rophe—*the Lord heals;* Yahweh Tsuri—*the Lord is my Rock*. Although God remains the same, each name describes a different attribute of his character. We relate to him based upon any number of these aspects. It's not a lot different than how we relate to other people. For example, my friend Scott holds an elected political position. But who he is comprises much more than that one aspect of his life, and other people relate to him accordingly:

- Someone who wants political advice might approach Scott as a politician.
- Someone seeking help in starting a business might come to Scott as a successful businessman.
- Maybe his friend Gary needs a golfing partner, so he approaches Scott as a golfer.
- Someone else is having a crisis in his personal life, so he comes to Scott as a friend or Christian brother.
- His son, Zach, needs some money, so he approaches Scott as Dad.

In all of these situations, Scott is the same person, but each circumstance reveals a different component of who he is. The more of these components we are familiar with, the better we know Scott.

In similar fashion, as our understanding of God's nature increases, not only is our worship deeply affected, but every facet of our relationship with him broadens. How? The more we know him, the greater our trust. Psalm 9:10 says, "Those who know your name will trust in you." The more we know him, the greater our effectiveness in prayer. Jesus said, "You may ask me for anything *in my name* and I will do it" (John 14:14, emphasis mine). The more we know him, the greater our sense of security and confidence. "I will protect him *because he acknowledges my name.* He will call upon me, and I will answer him; I will be with him in trouble, I will deliver him and honor him" (Psalm 91:14–15, emphasis mine).

As I said, there are many names for God in Scripture, but of all the names of God, no other is mentioned in Scripture more than Father. In the New Testament God is referred to as Father 267 times, 188 of those by Jesus. As the firstborn Son, Jesus revealed to all mankind that God is *our* Father, as well as his. When the disciples asked Jesus to teach them how to pray, he told them to begin with "our Father" (Matthew 6:9). From the start, he wanted them to approach God on the right and most important basis: he's our Father, our Dad, our Papa. This distinguishes Christianity from every other religion that has ever existed. Judaism comes the closest. However, even the Jews accused Jesus of blasphemy when he called himself the *Son* of God (Matthew 26:65). Muslims certainly don't see Allah as a father; other eastern religions don't even recognize a personal God, much less a personal God who is a father.

The implications of seeing God as our Father are staggering. John perceived it, and in 1 John 3:1 declared, "How great is the love the Father has lavished on us, that we should be called the children of God! And that is what we are!" The word "lavish" means to extend profusely or to be recklessly extravagant. Our being given the status of God's children brings an inexhaustible manifestation of his love towards us. Yet, many of us don't grasp it because of faulty views based on the relationship we've had with our earthly fathers. If our earthly fathers were emotionally distant, maybe harsh or abusive on the one hand or passive on the other, the word "father" may not carry a positive connotation. In fact, research shows that many prominent atheists—Nietzsche, Stalin, Hitler, even Madalyn Murray O'Hair—had fathers who were cruel or who died when they were young. So we need to look to the Bible to show us a description of the kind of father that God is.

I believe the parable of the prodigal son in Luke 15:11–32 paints a clear portrait of God as Father. In the parable, the younger son was tired of his father and his father's way of life. Filled with impertinence, he boldly approached his father and basically said, "I want my inheritance now so I can do with it what I want, when I want." Headstrong in his determination to satisfy himself, he took all of his belongings with him when he left. There was no way he would ever come back. His heartless rejection of his father was complete.

Soon the son had squandered all his inheritance. He had lived on the wild side, and when it all came crashing in, he found himself in a pigpen of misery. So he decided to return home. The best he could hope for was that his father would take him on as a hired hand. That's why he was totally unprepared for what he experienced when he rounded the bend—his father was actually running towards him! It would have been outrageous and humiliating for a Middle Eastern man to run in public wearing a long robe. But this father didn't care what people thought. Compassion for his son overrode all else.

This father was anything but emotionally distant. Barely waiting for his son to express repentance, he sent for a robe, signet ring, and sandals to restore his son's dignity and position. This father lavished on his son forgiveness, generosity, and comfort. He said, "Bring the fattened calf and kill it. Let's have a feast and celebrate. For this son of mine was dead and is alive again; he was lost and is found" (Luke 15:23–24).

Jesus says this is what our heavenly Father is like. He's not ashamed of us when we've blown it. Filled with tenderness and mercy, always watching and waiting for us to come home, our Father embraces us with a depth of acceptance that we find no place else. And that is a truth he wants us to discover. God is our *Abba Father* (Romans 8:15).

Truth #3: We Face a Fierce Enemy in the Battle for Truth.

There is another "father" we must contend with if we are to be resolved in holding fast to the truth. We must wage war against an enemy who is so characterized by deception that he is called "the father of lies" (John 8:44). His strategy hasn't changed much over the years. In the very beginning, he deceived Eve with half-truths and false accusations, resulting in her disobedience. When God asked her what she had done, she responded, "The serpent deceived me, and I ate" (Genesis 3:13). In the book of Revelation we find the same deceptive nature still operating. "He [the angel] seized the dragon, that ancient serpent, who is the devil, or Satan, and bound him for a thousand years. He threw him into the Abyss, and locked and sealed it over him, to keep him from deceiving the nations anymore…" (Revelation 20:2–3). The strongest assault on our freedom and legacy comes through the use of lies and deception.

It doesn't take a rocket scientist to recognize that truth is no longer "marching on" in our country. Although we may have been "conceived in liberty," we are now being "euthanized" by political correctness. The suppression of free speech began years ago on college campuses. Today it restricts anyone who voices a belief in absolutes. In almost every arena of life, our postmodern society denies the existence of any universal truth. Whether it's the teacher who's frowned upon because she refuses to teach evolution as fact or the politician who is painted as a bigot because he espouses marriage as a union between a man and a woman, standing against the tide of cultural relativism is becoming increasingly difficult. Even those places we look to as harbingers of truth and freedom, like the courts and the press, are faltering. Lawyers may suppress the truth, or even distort it, if it enhances their chance of winning a case. Honesty and commitment, once prerequisites of solid journalism, all too often have been replaced with standards like those expressed in the now infamous remark of former news anchor Dan Rather, "I don't think you have to always tell the truth to be honest."

Many businesses in our country owe their success to deception. Take the abortion industry, whose whole strategy lies in convincing the public that the "fetus" is a "choice not a child." I was perusing through the phone book the other day when I came across a quarter-page, color advertisement for American Healthcare Services. It pictured six smiling women with the caption: "We're Here for You." The rest of the ad read:

> Our friendly and courteous all female staff is dedicated to making your visit and decision comfortable. Our goal and

mission is to take good care of you. For caring help you can depend on, just call us now.

Offering:

- Abortions to 24 weeks
- Quick, easy, gentle
- Comfortably awake or asleep
- Very low fees

This sounded to me more like an advertisement for the Ramada Inn than an abortion clinic. Such is the nature of deception. Even the yellow pages can't be trusted!

God expects the church not only to be different, but also to *make* a difference. Jesus said, "You are the salt of the earth. But if the salt loses its saltiness, how can it be made salty again? It is no longer good for anything, except to be thrown out and trampled by men" (Matthew 5:13). If the church fails to preserve the standard of truth, who will? According to researcher George Barna, the salt may not even be making it to the shaker. He reports that although 85% of all adults in America claim that religious faith is very important in their lives, less than half who call themselves born-again Christians believe in absolute truth.[2] The church, in an increasingly desperate attempt to be relevant, seems to be replacing traditional values with those similar to the values of the culture. Such values include independence, personal happiness, tolerance, comfort, and instant gratification. The greater the church distances itself from the truth, the more it becomes a mere reflection of the world it is supposed to be influencing.

One of the most powerful deceptions we face in our country is masked in consumerism. It's the lie that we find freedom and satisfaction in things, things, and more things. Everything is viewed in terms of consumption. And it's pervasive. I don't think there's a store my son could walk into and not find something he wanted to buy. From a five-cent fireball at the drugstore to an iPod at Best Buy, he has definitely been affected by the lure of consumerism. One writer coined it well, "We no longer consume to live, but live to consume." Consumerism heralds the secular good news that the freedom to choose our "stuff" leads to happiness.

A proliferation of choices in every area of life has emerged to satisfy our demands for something new. That's why you can select from over 177 different shades of Revlon lipstick and why my small, local grocery store offers 151 varieties and sizes of potato chips. I counted them! We've grown so accustomed to the benefits of consumerism that, as Americans, the possibility of not having a choice in everything has become intolerable.

The truth expressed in Christianity diametrically opposes the cry of consumerism. Jesus preached that life consists of more than buying and selling. He emphasized the virtues of self-control, perseverance, and sacrifice, but these virtues find little room in a consumer mentality. Because personal comfort has become such a high commodity, pressure is brought on churches to change the emphasis in their messages. If they want to be *successful,* they should focus more on self-fulfillment than salvation from sin. Often referred to as the "McChurch mentality," God himself begins to be viewed as a consumer item to be brought out of the box when we are hurt, then put away when we no longer need him. Serve up a little cheap grace, high in pleasing the tastes of the people but low on substance and nutrients. Since consumerism is extremely individualistic, it's all about *you: your* needs, *your* desires, *your* gifts, and keeping *your* options open.

When Jesus talked about the end times, he basically said that the lies were going to be so impressive, packaged with such signs and wonders, that if possible, even believers would be deceived. "For false Christs and false prophets will appear and perform great signs and miracles to deceive even the elect—if that were possible" (Matthew 24:24). The elect, I believe, are those who steadfastly hold to the truth. It is not possible for those who are resolved in truth to be taken in by the lies. If we are to remain free, it is vital that we commit ourselves to fighting for the truth. God is looking for those in this generation who are willing to pledge their "lives," their "fortunes," and their "sacred honor" in order to leave the mark of truth.

Hold tight to truth
For if truth dies
Nothing else remains
But an endless tunnel of darkness.

Hold tight to love
For without love,
Truth's weight
Will tear the garment

The three truths I presented are only a few of the "self-evident truths" found in Christianity. Others are described in the following chapters. Truth pours the foundation on which all else is built. Without the mark of truth as a starting place, there's really no place else to go. Without the mark of truth, we will never progress to the next mark.

DIGGING DEEPER

1. What are some areas in your life that have been solved with resolve? Are there any areas that still need to be resolved?
2. Name a time when you resisted compromising the truth. What were the effects?
3. What are some "gods" you are tempted to put ahead of God?
4. Name something that has been added to you as a result of seeking God first.
5. What is your concept of a "father"? How does it compare to the description of the father in the parable of the prodigal son?
6. Name an area where "political correctness" has influenced you.
7. How have the cultural values of independence, personal happiness, instant gratification, and consumerism affected you?
8. What has been your reaction when not given a *choice* in something?
9. What are you "willing to pledge" in order to leave the mark of truth?

CHAPTER 2

WHY DO WE SAY NO?
THE MARK OF OBEDIENCE

The ability to accept God's unconditional grace and ferocious love is all
the fuel we need to obey him in return.
—Donald Miller
Blue Like Jazz

WHEN MY SON was entering into his teenage years, I once asked him what he thought of when I said the word "obey." His response was concise: "Mom."

"Mom?"

"Yeah, because you used that word, or some conjugation of it, so often when I was growing up," he explained.

I guess I did. I knew if he didn't catch the importance of a lifestyle characterized by obedience that he would suffer the consequences the rest of his life. He might leave a mark in the world, but not the one God intended.

I think most of us would consider obedience to God as not only virtuous but also beneficial. Scripture speaks clearly and frequently about the importance of being marked with obedience. Deuteronomy 28:1–2 states, "If you fully obey the Lord your God and carefully follow all his commands I give you today, the Lord your God will set you high above all the nations on earth. All these blessings will come upon you and accompany you if you obey the Lord your God." The next twelve verses describe the extent of some of those blessings.

- "You will be blessed in the city and blessed in the country."
- Your children, crops, and livestock will be blessed.
- You will have victory over your enemies.
- "You will always be at the top, never the bottom."

In contrast, Deuteronomy 28:15 makes clear what will happen as a result of disobedience. "However, if you do not obey the Lord your God and do not carefully follow all his commands and decrees I am giving you today, all these curses will come upon you and overtake you." The next *fifty-two* verses detail the curses encountered when the laws of the Lord are defied. That's right. Fifty-two verses are devoted to warning us about the consequences of disobedience. Perhaps that's a subtle commentary on how some of us are more likely motivated by the fear of pain than the promise of reward. Nevertheless, we see that a chief benefit of obedience is that it opens the way for the blessings of God.

Furthermore, the person marked with obedience enjoys the satisfaction of an ongoing, intimate relationship with Jesus. First John 2:3–5 states, "We know that we have come to know him if we obey his commands. The man who says, 'I know him,' but does not do what he commands is a liar, and the truth is not in him. But if anyone obeys his word, God's love is truly made complete in him. This is how we know we are in him."

Those are pretty strong words. If we want to know God better, we won't be able to unless we do what he tells us to do. It works something like this: Every time he gives us a directive, we have the opportunity to experience some aspect of his nature. You know what I mean. God directs you to give all the money you received from that speaking engagement to buy Bibles for soldiers in Iraq, and you become more aware of his generosity. You call someone and ask that person to meet for coffee, and during the two-hour conversation you feel like you have only succeeded in beating your head against a brick wall. You determine you'll never do that again. But God says to call once more. You do, and you are amazed at the depth of his grace. God directs you to pray for the restoration of a relationship. After five or six years and seemingly little movement, you're overwhelmed with his loving tenacity. In almost every situation, as we obey him, we come to know him more.

So, if it's through obedience that we receive the blessings of God and through obedience that we come to know him more intimately, being obedient shouldn't be a problem, right? Not quite. For us fallen creatures, obedience is never a slam dunk. We wrestle with this "free will" we've been given and constantly have to decide, in both big issues and small, whether we are going to obey God or follow our own agendas. We can come up with as many reasons why we shouldn't obey as there are people in the world, but I'd like to look at three particularly common excuses that feed our *résistance*.

Excuse #1: "I Can't."

This excuse focuses on what *we* can or cannot do. It confronts our unwillingness to be stretched. I saw an example of this the other day. I was babysitting for two children in our church, Gracie and Richard. A conflict had erupted, resulting in Gracie hitting Richard. So I told Gracie to apologize, and after a few coachings, she finally whispered, "Sorry, Richard." Then I instructed Richard to tell Gracie that he forgave her.

After a long pause, with all the sympathy he could muster in those big blue eyes, he sheepishly muttered, "I don't know how to say that."

Sometimes I think we're more like Richard than we care to admit. We confuse our abilities with our unwillingness. Obedience begins with willingness. Second Corinthians 8:12 says, "For if the willingness is there, the gift is acceptable according to what one has, not according to what he does not have." Although this passage refers to financial giving, the principle remains the same. God never asks us to do something that he won't help us do, even if it seems beyond our capability. Or as I've often heard a pastor friend of ours say, "God is looking for *availability* more than *ability*." Our availability could make the difference between life and death. Let's look at two scriptural examples, Esther and Gideon, to illustrate this point.

Right after Esther was selected to be the new queen in Persia, a decree was issued that all the Jews in the kingdom were to be slaughtered. When her uncle, Mordecai, asked Esther to go the king and intervene on the

Jews' behalf, she resisted. She knew that to go before the king without being summoned could result in her death, and she wasn't willing to put her life at risk. But Mordecai cut through her unwillingness. He said, "Do not think that because you are in the king's house you alone of all the Jews will escape. For if you remain silent at this time, relief and deliverance for the Jews will arise from another place, but you and your father's family will perish. And who knows but that you have come to royal position for such a time as this?" (Esther 4:13–14). Mordecai's admonition didn't fall on deaf ears. When Esther realized what was at stake, she took action. She called for all the Jews in the city, as well as her own maids, to fast and pray for her for three days. She was faced with a daunting task: saving all the Jews in the land. But she allowed herself to be available, even if it meant her death. She did what she could to enlist the power of God, and in the end, she was successful. God used her willingness to save her people.

The story of Gideon, as recorded in the book of Judges, chapters six and seven, further demonstrates how God uses availability over ability. The nation of Israel had been ravished by the Midianites for seven years—a consequence of Israel's disobedience. God, in his mercy, was now preparing to deliver them. He chose an unlikely vessel, Gideon, to be his instrument. An angel appeared to Gideon and gave him what seemed like *mission impossible.* To paraphrase, Gideon argued, "Me? I can't do that. I'm the least in my family, and my clan is the weakest in Manasseh. You've got the wrong guy." Of course, God didn't have the wrong guy, and after several miraculous signs and the assurance that God would be with him, Gideon was finally convinced. The task actually was too big for him alone, but God told him that he would use Gideon's availability to accomplish his purpose if Gideon would "go in the strength [he] had" (Judges 6:14). Gideon obeyed, and God kept his promise. Gideon led Israel to complete victory over the Midianite army.

Recently I read the book *1776* by David McCullough. Although we think of the year 1776 as a glorious year, with the Declaration of Independence and the birth of our nation, in reality it was a hard, brutal, discouraging time. It was a year of sustained suffering, disease, desertion, and disillusionment. George Washington himself had never led an army in battle, and he was going up against the most powerful, well-equipped country in the world. In addition, trained mercenaries from Germany, the Hessians, had joined Britain, and many of the people living in this country were still loyal to England, so they fought against the patriots as well. Given the strength of opposition, Washington easily could have said, "I can't possibly lead this rag-tag army to victory." He faced defeat after defeat, retreat after retreat, until the British were threatening to enter Philadelphia. Even some of Washington's most trusted officers began to doubt his capability in securing victory. But if Washington doubted his abilities, it was never known. What is known is that he never wavered in his willingness to answer the call of duty, no matter how bleak or inglorious.

Finally, on December 26, the patriots won the Battle of Trenton, followed by the Battle of Princeton, and the tide of the war began to change. McCullough writes, "Without Washington's leadership and unrelenting perseverance, the revolution almost certainly would have failed. He was not a brilliant strategist, or tactician, not a gifted orator, not an intellectual. At several crucial moments he had shown marked indecisiveness. He had made serious mistakes in judgment.... But he learned steadily from experience. Above all, Washington never forgot what was at stake and he never gave up."[3]

God may not be asking us to save a nation, but the issue of our willingness to obey rather than say "I can't" is essential in the fulfilling of his plans. When we feel a nudge from the Lord, rather than asking "why me?" we should be asking "why not me?"

Excuse #2: "It's Too Hard."

This excuse focuses not so much on our unwillingness, but on the difficulty of the circumstances. It confronts our lack of perseverance. Trials are sometimes the hardest places to walk in obedience because they require us to keep at it long after we want to quit.

The book of James refers to Job as an example of one who persevered, so let's look at Job. Job was a wealthy man who lost all his livestock, servants, and children. How did he respond? It's recorded in Job 1:20–22 that "...he fell to the ground in worship and said: 'Naked I came from my mother's womb, and naked I will depart. The Lord gave and the Lord has taken away; may the name of the Lord be praised.' In all this,

Job did not sin by charging God with wrongdoing." Job passed the test. He didn't join the Accuser (see Rev. 12:10) in condemning God of wrongdoing. So, did he receive the blessings of obedience? Not yet.

In chapter two Job got another test. Painful sores erupted all over his body. The severity of the affliction so distorted his appearance, that he literally became unrecognizable. He was forced to scrape the festering wounds with pieces of broken pottery as he sat on a deserted ash heap. At this point, his wife told him to curse God and die. But, again, he refused to blame God. "You are talking like a foolish woman. Shall we accept good from God, and not trouble? In all this, Job did not sin in what he said" (Job 2:10). He passed two tests. So now did he receive the blessings of obedience? *No!* He had to persevere through thirty-five more chapters before God spoke to him. The challenge of perseverance didn't even start until after he had passed the tests.

After we have passed a test, how often are we tempted to think, "OK, where's my reward?" Sometimes the reward comes, but sometimes (actually quite often), God wants to do a bigger work in us. That was the outcome for Job. In the end, not only did he receive back twice as much as he had lost, but he also came to *see* God. "My ears had heard of you but now my eyes have seen you" (Job 42:5). The revelation was so profound that Job was moved to a depth of repentance that he had never before experienced. He was transformed because he saw God in a whole new light. And that vision completed him as a man.

I believe it is the ongoing nature of our trials that becomes the real testing ground as to whether or not we will bear the mark of obedience—because it is there where we are tempted most to see God in the wrong light, there where we are enticed to join the accuser. Then our mischaracterization of God conveniently affords us the perfect reason why we shouldn't obey. But if we obediently persevere through our troubles, we will find, as Job did, maturity, completeness, and a new vision of God. Author Stephen Hill writes, "It is during the raging battle the soldier is tested. During these times we must trust. He uses the dark, difficult trials of our lives to make us into vessels for his honor."[4]

Perseverance insists that we remain steadfast. Perseverance means it's not over until the proverbial "fat lady sings." The cost of not pressing on, even when victory seems assured, can be high. Just ask Penn State football coach, Joe Paterno.

It had been a hard-fought football game between Penn State and Michigan. Finally, PSU scored in the last fifty-three seconds to pull ahead by four points. They kicked off the return to Michigan. I guess the defense thought they had already won, because Michigan met little resistance as they ran down the field, getting ever closer to the PSU goal line. Although the Penn State defense may have been sleeping, one person who was not asleep was Lloyd Carr, the Michigan coach. He called a time out, and when the players went back on the field, he didn't think the right time had been recorded on the clock. So he argued with the refs to put four seconds back; they relented by restoring two. Michigan was lined up at the goal line. With one second left on the board, they completed a pass and won the game (much to the chagrin of many of us in the crowd, I might add).

As long as we live on this earth, we cannot afford to coast. We have an opponent who is far more relentless than the best of football coaches. The accuser is determined to keep us from the goal that God has for us. But as we resist thinking that God's assignments are too hard or that we don't need to persevere, the fruit of obedience will begin to leave its mark.

Excuse # 3: "I Don't Love God Enough."

This last excuse is the most revealing, but the one we are most apt to conceal from even ourselves. This excuse, "I don't love God enough," exposes our lack of gratitude. In spite of all that God has done for us, we still don't love him enough to do what he asks. Ignatius wrote, "It seems to me in light of the Divine Goodness…that ingratitude is the most abominable of sins." In her insightful book *Radical Gratitude*, Ellen Vaughn observes that many believers seem to look for life principles that are a bit more "spiritually sexy" than gratitude.[5] They want something more exciting, more dramatic. But a lack of gratitude not only undermines the very basis of our worship, it also obliterates the mark of obedience.

When we fail to thank God for all he's done and for all the opportunities he's given us, when we stop appreciating his patience, mercy, and provision, we inevitably start to rebel. "For although they knew God, they neither glorified him as God nor *gave thanks to him,* but their thinking became futile and their foolish hearts were darkened" (Romans 1:21, emphasis mine). The scripture says that the reason they stopped being thankful was that they *suppressed the truth.* They stopped acknowledging God's divinity, his power, his greatness. They shifted the focus of their adoration to created things rather than the Creator. The consequences were dire: "They have become filled with every kind of wickedness, evil, greed and depravity. They are full of envy, murder, strife, deceit and malice. They are gossips, slanders, God-haters, insolent, arrogant and boastful; they invent ways of doing evil; they disobey their parents; they are senseless, faithless, heartless, ruthless" (Romans 1:29–31). Their degeneracy was initiated with a lack of thanks!

The ultimate motivation for our obedience should rise from a profound sense of gratitude for what Christ has done. If we are Christians, we have been delivered from more than we'll ever know in this life. And we have the opportunity to live the richest, fullest existence we could possibly imagine. We're missing the point if our obedience stems from some legalistic mindset. We obey him not because we have to, but because we are so thankful for all he has done. Gratitude cultivates love, and love cultivates obedience. John 14:23–24 says, "If anyone loves me, he will obey my teaching…he who does not love me will not obey my teaching." There is no excuse any of us could give that would justify not obeying the Lord.

It was around 1977 when Chip and I embarked on one of the most significant walks of obedience in our lives. We had been married four years and had dreams of going to Alaska after Chip finished the job of restoring the old family farmhouse. But our plans changed after I read a book that mentioned a little-known Christian community called L'Abri, where people could go to study and find answers to basic questions about God, life, and everything in between. It was located in an obscure village in Switzerland. We felt the Lord directing us to pack up everything and leave for an undetermined amount of time. In those days, few people in the States, including us, had heard of Francis Schaeffer, the director of L'Abri. So it was definitely a walk of faith. We had no idea what to expect; we just knew that we were to go.

We saved our money, finding out only a few weeks before we were to leave that most of our savings would have to be used to actually stay at L'Abri. So we made plans to fly stand-by on Icelandic Airlines. It was the cheapest airfare we could find, but even with that, we had to spend the first night sleeping on the floor of the JFK airport until seats opened up on the next flight!

We finally arrived in Luxembourg, where we caught a train that would take us through France and on to Switzerland. We purchased tickets that would get us half way, the plan being to spend the night somewhere in France and then complete the trip to Switzerland the next day. Unfortunately, we were unaccustomed to the punctuality of European trains, and when we reached our destination, by the time we loaded up two large backpacks and a guitar, the train was pulling off! Stifling the impulse to make a daring leap, we made it back to our seats and decided to hop off at the next station as quickly as possible. However, it was dark now, and when the train pulled into the next stop, there was nothing but a deserted platform in the middle of nowhere. So we opted to remain on the train, praying frantically, wondering how we were ever going to explain our predicament to the French-speaking conductor.

In the meantime, we happened to meet an American girl who was getting off at Basel, a fairly large city. She was staying with some friends-of-some-friends, and offered to ask them if they knew of a place where we might stay for the night. The train pulled in (somehow we had managed to escape the conductor's eye), and the girl located her contacts. They informed us that they knew of one place that might be available, and they even offered to drive us there. But they weren't sure we would like it—it was a *Christian* hotel. Chuckling to ourselves, we said we thought that would be fine.

That was just the beginning of how the Lord would show us his faithfulness in our days at L'Abri. Not only did we acquire an intellectual basis for our faith (and make wonderful friends), but also the many ways that God provided for us laid a foundation that we would need as we followed the call God had placed on our lives.

Dr. and Mrs. Schaeffer's pursuit of truth had led them to respond in the only way possible for people of integrity...with obedience. Dr. Schaeffer often challenged us to become—as they had become— seeds willing to fall to the ground and die in order to yield fruit for the Lord.

After our time at L'Abri, I remember remarking to Chip on our way back to the States, "I always thought Christianity was true, but not *this true*." One small step of obedience, to leave everything and everyone we knew to travel to an unfamiliar destination for an uncertain reason, was a risk we were willing to take. What we received in return, as they say in the commercials, was priceless.

The mark of obedience that we saw in the Schaeffers' lives was the key to their influence. This influence was felt directly through their many books and lectures and their way of life, but also indirectly through the countless numbers of people they affected who in turn have written, lectured, and lived godly lives. Influence is yet another mark God wants to embed in his followers.

DIGGING DEEPER

1. In the context of Deuteronomy 28, name some of the blessings of obedience that you've experienced.
2. When was a time that obedience taught you something about God's nature?
3. What is your most common excuse for saying "no" to God?
4. Was there a time when God asked you to do something and you said, "I can't"? How about a time when you thought you couldn't but said "yes" anyway? What were the results in both cases?
5. Describe a time when it took perseverance in order to obey a command of God.
6. What are some specific areas in your life for which you have *radical gratitude*?

CHAPTER 3

PROPHETIC, POWERFUL, AND PASSIONATE

THE MARK OF INFLUENCE

> *Never reserve anything. Pour out the best you have and always be poor.*
> *Never be diplomatic and careful about the treasure God gives.*
> —Oswald Chambers
> *My Utmost for His Highest*

A FEW YEARS ago at a class reunion, I ran into one of my old high school chums, Johnny Hoover. Johnny grew up dirt poor, but after graduation he had entered the military and gone on to become a highly successful businessman. As we chatted, he expressed how happy he was to see me again because he wanted to thank me for the influence I'd had on his life. He said he had never forgotten the confidence I instilled in him to "make something of his life." Shocked, I think I blurted out, "Who, me?" I was stunned to think my affirmation had produced such an effect. Johnny went on to say that the most satisfying moments of his whole career had come when he had been given the opportunity to encourage others as I'd encouraged him. His remarks were the high point of the evening....

Whether we realize it or not, God has created his people to enjoy the mark of influence. Perhaps you've heard the story of Telemachus. Telemachus was a monk from Asia who lived in the fifth century. He embraced an ascetic life filled with praying, studying, and caring for the vegetable garden at the monastery. Then one day as he was praying, he felt the Lord directing him to go to Rome. He didn't know why he was to go, but he knew the voice of the one sending him. So in obedience he set off, believing the Lord would reveal the purpose of his direction once he got there.

Upon arriving, he found himself following the large, noisy crowds to the Coliseum. Bewilderment flooded through him as he realized what was taking place. Gladiators armed with piercing steel swords were fighting to the death for the *pure entertainment* of the crowd.

Overcome with such low regard for human life, Telemachus jumped to his feet and rushed into the arena, boldly shouting, "In the name of Christ, forbear!" Ignored by the gladiators and jeered by the crowd, this scrawny servant of God would not yield. "In the name of Christ, forbear!" he shouted a second time. With seemingly no thought of his own peril, he tried to put himself between the two men, and he cried a third time, "In the name of Christ, forbear!"

By now the blood-lusting multitude was incensed. Who was this puny distracter getting in the way of their amusement? Filled with rage, one by one they began hurling stones at Telemachus, crushing his fragile body until it was *his* blood that soaked the sand, *his* life that was forfeited for their pleasure. But his sacrifice was not in vain. A hush fell over the stadium as the spectators viewed his motionless form lying lifeless on the ground. The arena began to empty as a conscience-stricken crowd sought to escape the brutal scene.

Telemachus' death marked the last gladiatorial game that would ever be held in the Coliseum. His courage stirred the Emperor to decree an end to one of the most savage, vicious forms of entertainment the world has ever known.

Although I've read the story of Telemachus on numerous occasions, I am still moved at how God used a little, unknown peasant to help shut down the massive cult of violence in the Roman Empire.

Telemachus bore the mark of influence. Three elements comprised that influence:

1) Prayer—it was through prayer that God directed him to go to Rome.

2) Courage—he was fearless in speaking boldly.
3) Undying love for Christ—it gave him the motivation to sacrifice his own life for the sake of truth.

I find these same elements in Ephesians 6:18–20, 24: "And pray in the Spirit on all occasions with all kinds of prayers and requests, with this in mind, be alert and always keep on praying for all the saints. Pray also for me, that whenever I open my mouth, words may be given me so that I will fearlessly make known the mystery of the gospel, for which I am an ambassador in chains. Pray that I may declare it fearlessly as I should.... Grace to all who love our Lord Jesus with an undying love."

Whether God draws us to make an impact on a single individual, like Johnny Hoover, or a whole culture, as Telemachus did, we each have been given the opportunity to bear the mark of influence—prophetic, powerful, passionate influence. The passage in Ephesians outlines how God engraves that mark of influence on our lives:

- Prophetic influence –born out of prayer (verse 18)
- Powerful influence—born out of courage (verses 19–20)
- Passionate influence—born out of an undying love for Jesus (verse 24)

Let's explore these three types of influence further.

Prophetic Influence Through Prayer

Ephesians 6:18 says, "And pray in the spirit on all occasions with all kinds of prayers and requests. With this in mind, be alert and always keep on praying for all the saints." To pray *in the spirit* is to pray prophetically. It is God-directed prayer. It influences the whole realm of the spirit because it involves participation in a spiritual battle in the heavenlies. Interestingly, the verses that precede verse eighteen have to do with spiritual warfare—standing against rulers, authorities, powers, and spiritual forces of evil. Paul is saying to put on the full armor of God and to pray because *it will make a difference*. The secret behind effective, prophetic prayer begins with *knowing* it will make a difference, that

God has entrusted us with authority—authority that is to be exercised to overcome the evil effects of the enemy on this earth.

I like the way the King James Version translates James 5:16: "the effectual fervent prayer of a righteous man avails much." The prayers of the righteous *avail much.* That means that something happens when the righteous pray that otherwise wouldn't have happened without the prayers. God is sovereign. But in his omniscience, he has ordained an open and not a closed universe. We do not act out predetermined parts. God has designed it that some things will happen only in answer to prayer (See 2 Chronicles 7:14; Job 42:8; Mark 9:29; James 5:15; 17-18). Heaven affects earth, but earth also affects heaven, so he invites us to participate with him in writing history. And that participation begins with prayer, because it is through prayer that we discern the will of God.

It is precisely because prayer has such a powerful effect, that Satan tries everything he can to keep us from grasping that truth. He knows that God has given us authority over him. First John 4:4 says, "Greater is he that is in you than he that is in the world." His only recourse, then, is to deceive us into thinking we don't have authority. If we don't believe we have the authority through prayer to make a difference, we won't use it. We'll be constricted to generic prayers, like "God bless this food" and "Give us a good day." Certainly, there's nothing wrong with praying that God will bless our food and give us a good day, but if that's the essence of our prayers, we won't go far in influencing our world. Don't be afraid to *pray big*!

In his book *That None Should Perish*, Ed Silvoso explains that we have compromised the biblical truth of *who we are* and *what we are meant to accomplish.* Instead of approaching the throne of God with confidence— like a beloved child given wondrous tasks— we lose sight of the reason we are on the earth. He writes, "We are so afraid of embarrassing God with prayers he might not answer that we have ceased to pray for miracles.... Our prayers seem to be written by lawyers who qualify every sentence to provide God with a way out in case no answer comes."[6]

Prophetic prayer relies on both the Word of God and the Holy Spirit. Without the Word, there is no substance to our faith and therefore no power to our prayers. When I use the Scripture as the basis for my prayers, I sense an authority that is not otherwise present. My faith is activated, and I pray with greater confidence and assurance. But sometimes, I don't know specifically how to pray or what to pray for. It is in those times that I depend upon the assistance of the Holy Spirit.

The other morning as I walked in the front door, my eighty-three-year-old mother was sitting at the kitchen table. I was surprised because she had been sick with pneumonia the last few days and pretty much confined to bed. Upon seeing me, she began to cough so severely that she couldn't get her breath. Her eyes widened in panic as she pointed to her throat and tried to mouth the words, "I can't breathe." The mucous in her bronchial tubes was so thick that it was literally suffocating her.

As we waited anxiously for the ambulance to arrive, she would get through one coughing spasm, only to have another episode. There was no time to *think* about how to pray. All I could do was let the Holy Spirit intercede with "groans that words cannot express" (Romans 8:26). He helped me to pray when my thoughts and words failed. My faith was fortified.

That night, as I tucked Mom into bed, she said, "There was a battle today between God and Satan, and God won." I agreed. The victory had come through prayer.

Given the powerful effectiveness of prayer, we are exhorted to "pray on all occasions with all kinds of prayers" (Ephesians 6:18). First Timothy 2:1, 3–4 says, "I urge then, first of all, that requests, prayer, intercession and thanksgiving be made for everyone. This is good and pleases God our Savior who wants all men to be saved...."

Each of us has a sphere that God wants us to influence through prayer. Yours is different from mine and mine from yours. We have different family members, co-workers, neighbors, and friends. *God wants everyone in our sphere to be saved.*

Not long after my dad received the Lord (at age 65) he began to keep a prayer journal to list the names of people he knew who were in need of God. He recently showed me his compilation of over 600 names he has prayed for on a regular basis. Beside many of those names, well over half, was written the word "yes." Those were the ones who had accepted Christ.

Our prayers make such a difference! Be generous in sowing prayer for those in your sphere. Don't be afraid to ask people if you can pray for them. God wants to meet their needs in a way that reveals both his power and love.

Recognizing how much prayer can influence the lives of those around me has accelerated my passion for prayer in a number of ways. I changed our answering machine to ask people to leave a prayer request if we aren't home. One day, I felt the Lord direct me to go see a neighbor who had recently lost his sight in a car accident. I had nothing specific to say, but I knew I could offer to pray, which he gladly received. He is now getting his sight back, and I believe my prayers played a part in the answer. On another occasion, I was talking with a different neighbor who was complaining about his landlord. I knew this neighbor wasn't a believer, but I told him I would pray for the situation. The next time I saw him, he reported, to his delight, that things had worked out. Not only did he acknowledge gratitude for my prayers, but he also enlisted my prayers for another situation involving a teacher at his child's school!

We should be ready to pray at any moment, anywhere, anytime. Consider when someone asks you to pray for a concern, joining with them at that moment. Don't wait for a later time and risk forgetting. Scripture tells us that the unity of two or three in prayer is powerful. But it is also vital to have those alone, set-aside times with the Lord when we can't be distracted or disturbed.

We recently established a prayer room at our church, available 24/7. It is key code accessible so that people in the church are able to come and pray any time. The room has soft lights, a cross, a CD player, and a request board. Lovingly referred to by some as the "prayer nazi" because I'm always encouraging people to participate, I feel like some weeks I live in the prayer room. There is an intimacy with the Lord in that atmosphere, and nothing in my Christian life has been quite like it in drawing me closer to him and furthering my conviction concerning the power of prayer.

If we hope to be people of influence, it begins on our knees.

Powerful Influence Through Courage

Ephesians 6:19–20 states, "Pray also for me that whenever I open my mouth, words may be given me so that I will *fearlessly* make known the mystery of the gospel, for which I am an ambassador in chains. Pray that I may declare it fearlessly *as I should*" (emphasis mine). Paul asserts that he *should* be able to declare *fearlessly* what God has done. It may take courage to do that. That's why he's asking for prayer, because it doesn't necessarily come easily—for him or for us.

Courage encompasses a mental or moral strength to withstand danger or difficulty. One of my heroes is the late Aleksandr Solzhenitsyn, the Russian dissident who was exiled to our country before Communism fell in the Soviet Union. On coming to our country, he remarked: "A decline in courage may be the most striking feature an outside observer notices in the West in our days…particularly noticeable among the ruling and intellectual elites."[7] He said this at a lecture at Harvard. One has to wonder whether it took more courage for him to stand up to the intellectual elite there or to the Communist regime in his homeland!

Sadly, this "uncourageous" mindset to which Solzhenitsyn referred has taken a toll on the church. The church's mentality in the last few years has been more one of trying to accommodate the culture than of standing up to it in *loving* confrontation (the loving part is imperative). We're afraid we're going to be labeled as "judgmental" if we speak the truth. We want people to like us to the point that we are willing to compromise. Tolerance has superseded all other virtues and intolerance all vices. But intolerance for things which should not be tolerated reflects true courage, as pastor Keith Tucci illustrated in a unique way. He, with the help of his Team Redeem students, designed a t-shirt that says on the front, "Intolerance is a Beautiful Thing." The back of the t-shirt lists men and women whose lives illustrated this quality:

Frederick Douglass ....*intolerant* of slavery
Susan B. Anthony...................*intolerant* of only men voting
Amy Carmichael ....*intolerant* of child prostitution
Winston Churchill ....*intolerant* of Hitler
Lech Walesa............................*intolerant* of Communism
Mother Teresa ....*intolerant* of abortion

Don't be confused about tolerance. British author Dorothy Sayers said it well, "In the world it is called *tolerance* but in hell it is called *despair*, the sin that believes in nothing, cares for nothing, seeks to know nothing, interferes with nothing, enjoys nothing, hates nothing, finds purpose in nothing, lives for nothing, and remains alive because there is nothing for which it will die."[8]

So how do we regain this high ground that has been lost? How do we become bold and courageous in the midst of a mocking, sometimes hostile environment? How do we resist the fear of being labeled "judgmental" as we embrace this deeper call? If you are at all like me, you probably don't feel very courageous. But here are three suggestions that may help us cultivate courage:

1) Courage begins with everyday faithfulness.

Courage is not something exemplified only in Harrison Ford or Jack Bauer (any *24* fans?). It is developed through our everyday actions, because it is in the everyday that the kind of character courage necessitates is built. We may think our lives are mundane and ordinary, but there is a greater connection between the ordinary and the extraordinary than we think. Pascal prayed that he would be able to "do small things as if they were great, because of the Majesty of Christ, who does them in us and lives our life, and do great things as if they were small and easy because of His almighty power." [9] You see, courage calls to us in more places than on the front lines of battle. For example:

- It takes courage to look at the truth about ourselves. We have well-constructed self images, and it takes *guts* to acknowledge our jealousy, pride, hypocrisy, and self-centeredness.
- It takes courage to let go of grown children when they tell you they are moving (with your grandchildren) to Texas—and you live in Pennsylvania.
- It takes courage not to join in the office gossip.
- It takes courage to admit a mistake.
- It takes courage to expose the childhood abuse that you received.
- It takes courage, sometimes, just to maintain our trust in God when our ashes have not yet been transformed into beauty.

Whether or not we would ever rise to a single act of bravery is determined by how we live out these everyday areas of faithfulness. It makes me think of hobbits. J.R.R. Tolkien created hobbits as ordinary creatures faithfully doing ordinary things. But when called upon, they exhibited courage in remarkable ways. It was their faithfulness and reliability in ordinary life that enabled them to rise to the extraordinary when it came. Frodo, the main hobbit in *The Lord of the Rings*, never imagined that he would be instrumental in saving all of Middle Earth from the encroaching evil. But his moral fiber, developed through the *everyday*, had equipped him to resist the pull of power and qualified him to bravely face the challenge. What lesson can we learn from this? Don't underestimate the seemingly small things in your life. You may be being groomed for things you never thought possible. The one who is faithful in little, will be faithful in much (Matthew 25:23).

2) Courage is cultivated by running *to* rather than *away* from our fears.

Sometimes the only way to overcome our fear of doing something is to just do it. For me, the fear of not doing something has at times loomed larger than the fear of doing it—compelling me to take some action. For example, when my son, Josiah, was around five or six years old, I became bothered by some of the magazine covers on the newsstands at the grocery store check-out. *Cosmopolitan,* especially, always pictured a woman in some stage of undress. And it was right at Josiah's eye level. I really didn't want to confront the owner about it. I guess I was afraid he might think I was a religious nut or legalistic killjoy. But it continued to bug me, so finally I said, "OK, Lord, if this is you, let me see Mr. Herr alone somewhere in the store." Imagine the flip in my stomach when I turned up the next aisle and saw him packing the frozen foods.

With a bit of trepidation, I approached Mr. Herr and expressed my concern. He slightly brushed me off, but he did say he would look into it. A couple weeks passed, and the magazines were still there in all their glory. Again, I asked the Lord if I was to pursue, and again, I felt the gentle nudge: "*Take some copies and put them on his desk.*" So I dropped three magazines with pictures of half-naked ladies in his office, with a note explaining my continued unease with such *near-pornographic* displays. It took a few more confrontations, but eventually, *Cosmopolitan* was covered with cardboard.

In this situation, I had been afraid to do the right thing, but my fear of not doing something, once I knew the Lord was directing me, weighed heavier, so *I just did it*. That leads me to the third aid in cultivating courage.

3) Courage requires our knowing that God is with us.

Many scriptures reveal this principle. In Deuteronomy 31, the Israelites are being sent to take the Promised Land. They're approaching their first battle and the Lord speaks: "Be strong and courageous. Do not be afraid or terrified because of them *for the Lord your God goes with you...*" (Deuteronomy 31:6, emphasis mine). In 2 Chronicles 20, a coalition of enemies comes to make war on Israel. King Jehoshaphat knows he is outnumbered, and he cries out in despair. God responds, "Go out to face them tomorrow *and the Lord will be with you*" (verse 17, emphasis mine). Just as he promised, God was with them. The enemy was defeated in both cases (and in many more as well). When Jesus gave his *eleven* disciples the overwhelming task of making disciples of *all* nations, what words did he leave with them to instill courage? "And surely *I am with you always*, to the very end of the age" (Matthew 28:20, emphasis mine).

Knowing God is with us cuts through our fears and insecurities, making room for bravery to flourish. Ask God to give you opportunities to courageously speak the truth. You have the "hope of glory" (Colossians 1:27) in you. That's what the Bible says. Because of Christ within, whenever you walk into a room you should be thinking, "The hope of glory just entered." He wants us to walk in confidence and courage *as we should*.

Passionate Influence Through an Undying Love for Christ

Ephesians 6:24 says, "Grace to all who love our Lord Jesus Christ with an undying love." Prayer is imperative, courage crucial, but without an undying love for Christ, they are void of eternal influence.

To paraphrase Macbeth, courage without love is "… full of sound and fury, signifying nothing."

Love for God was the source of Israel's protection. "I remember the devotion of your youth, how as a bride you loved me and followed me through the desert…all who devoured her were held guilty and disaster overtook them" (Jeremiah 2:2–3). The enemy could not prevail over Israel because she was sold out to God. But before long, the people started turning to other gods and became slaves to other nations. In Hosea 13:3, he says Israel's love was like the morning mist that disappears like the dew. *Hardly undying.* It had evaporated as the nation began drinking the tainted water of the surrounding cultures. Consequently, Israel lost her influence.

What about our devotion? Have we, like Israel, or like the church in Ephesus (see Revelation 2:4), "lost our first love"? Have we become enamored by the world and diluted our passion for Christ? Has disappointment or busyness or just the tediousness of life stolen our fervor for him? We are told clearly in Matthew 24:12 that because of the increase of wickedness in the last days, the love of *most* will grow cold. I don't know about you, but that's one majority I don't want to be included in. That increase of wickedness will consist of persecution of believers, betrayal, and rampant deception—not an atmosphere where love thrives. Only those who stand firm to the end and do not deny their love for Christ will be saved.

But how do we stand firm to the end? How do we stay in love with Christ? What's the secret that prepares us for this kind of future? If we are challenged today by circumstances much less dire than these, how can we hope to remain faithful when everything around us starts to fall? The answer is: by remaining *firmly fixed* on God's love. We must always remind ourselves and each other of the lavishness of his heart towards us. His love for us is undying, and the way we cultivate an undying love for him is to take the love he offers us, embrace it, and let it transform us into his likeness.

I think that's what happened to Mary of Bethany. It seems that every time we read about Mary, she's at Jesus' feet. When Jesus first visited the home where she and her sister, Martha, lived, Martha was busy making all kinds of preparations. But not Mary; she was sitting *at the Lord's feet*, drinking in every word he said. Martha complained that Mary was slacking off, but Jesus defended her. He explained that it was Mary who was occupied with what was most important (Luke 10:39–42).

When Jesus returned to Bethany after Lazarus, their brother, had died, both sisters were heartbroken and distressed that Jesus had not come in time to heal him. Mary was so distraught that even when she heard that Jesus had arrived, she stayed behind. But when Martha relayed that Jesus was asking for her, she promptly got up and hurried to where he was. When she saw him, *she fell at his feet* (John 11:32, emphasis mine).

Six days before the Passover, Jesus attended a dinner given in his honor at their home. Maybe it was to celebrate Lazarus' resurrection. Whatever the occasion, Martha was serving, as usual; Lazarus was reclined with others at the table; Mary was doing neither. She had taken a pint of pure nard and was pouring it on *Jesus' feet* and wiping them with her hair (John 12:3). The perfume was so expensive, that it was worth *a year's wages*. That's comparable today to maybe $30,000…$40,000…$60,000? Even if Mary was wealthy, it would have been a costly gift. But Mary didn't care about how much it cost. She didn't care that the disciples rebuked her for not using the money to help the poor. She didn't care that it was the servants' job to wash feet. She didn't care that it was unseemly for a respectable woman to unbind her hair in public. She had an *undying love* for Jesus. She knew there was no devotion she could give him that was too extravagant.

Six days later, those feet were brutally nailed to the cross for her sins. She had sat at those feet, wept at those feet, washed and anointed those feet. Prophetically, she had been the one to prepare those feet for burial. Mary's undying love for Christ proclaims a passionate influence that continues to inspire over two thousand years later.

God wants you to leave a prophetic, powerful, passionate mark of influence in this world. Don't be deceived into thinking that because you don't hold an important position or possess a lot of resources that you are called to anything less. The world needs your mark of influence. Remember Telemachus. God will use your prayers, your courage, and your undying love for him to engrave a mark of influence that will last long after you have left the earth.

As senseless violence, deception, and injustice increasingly mars our society, a desperate plea for help cries out from the chaos. Those who bear the mark of influence are the ones who hear the cries and rescue those longing to be delivered from death. They are the ones who bear also the mark of life.

DIGGING DEEPER

1. Describe the part prayer plays in your life.
2. Give some examples of where prayer has clearly made a difference.
3. Who are some people in your sphere that God may want you to influence? What are you going to do about it?
4. What are some areas in your life in which you should show *intolerance*?
5. Name a situation you've experienced that required courage.
6. What are some things you do intentionally to "stay in love" with Christ?
7. Do you consider yourself to have more of a "Martha" or "Mary" mindset? How does this affect your relationship with Christ?
8. How would you like to influence the world?

CHAPTER 4

GIVE ME JESUS OR GIVE ME DEATH
THE MARK OF LIFE

At the moment a gun and a Bible have a few things in common. Both are small, black, have an immediate heft and are dangerous—the first to life, the second to the culture of death.

—Peggy Noonan
Wall Street Journal

THE TERM "CULTURE of death" was first coined in an address by Pope John Paul II. It refers to the devaluation of life that has flooded the world in recent years. We are bombarded with violence at every stage of life, from a mother's womb to high schools to abuse of the elderly. It has spread from the streets of New York City to quiet Amish families in Pennsylvania. In our country alone, suicides have doubled in the past ten years, predominantly among children. The media inundates us with images of life being carelessly blown away. How did we get to this point? Is there a way out? Can we escape this "culture of death" or are we doomed?

A child of the 60s generation, I was a graduate student at the University of Colorado in the 70s. Boulder at that time was the mecca of the counterculture. Anti-war protests, panhandlers, and dope filled the streets. I remember walking back to my apartment after my first venture to "the Hill," which at that time was the hub for hippies, shops, and all kinds of countercultural happenings. A straggly-looking fellow followed me halfway home, which wouldn't have been too upsetting had he not been *barking* the whole time. It was a fascinating place to be.

Out of the era of the 70s, a philosophy emerged that *nothing* was worth dying for. Life was to be experienced *now*. No country, no religion, not freedom, not democracy—nothing—was of more value than living for the moment. Thirty years later, the fruit of saying that nothing is worth dying for has resulted in an underlying notion that nothing is worth living for. I believe that is, in part, how we got here. But we don't have to stay this way.

The answer to not succumbing to the *culture of death* lies with the church. "For we are to God the aroma of Christ among those who are being saved and those who are perishing. To the one we are the smell of death; to the other, the fragrance of life" (2 Corinthians 2:15–16). As Christians, we are commissioned to put an end to the culture of death by exuding the mark of life. Jesus demonstrated that there *are* things worth dying for, that *we* are worth dying for. In Revelation 12:11, it's recorded that the ones who overcame were those who "did not love their lives so much as to shrink from death." Because they knew there was something far greater than the moment, these brave souls earned an inheritance of life. But today's church has been drinking from the same polluted stream as the rest of the world. We are affected by the culture of death more than we realize. And all too often, we fail to understand the importance of what we have to offer. God's plan has always been for his people to mark their surroundings with life. In order to do that, it is important that we recognize the characteristics of our inheritance, understand the forces that oppose us, and count the cost.

Characteristics of the Inheritance of Life

I think many of us either take for granted or simply don't understand the life-saving nature of our birthright. Psalm 16:5–11 identifies some of the characteristics of our inheritance. It says we have a "delightful inheritance," essentially because God has made known to us "the path of life" for the present as well as for eternity. Each verse addresses a particular feature of life—a feature that, if applied, will counter the culture of death. Let's look more closely at these verses.

Psalm 16:5–6 says, "Lord, you have assigned me my portion and my cup; you have made my lot secure. The boundary lines have fallen for me in pleasant places; surely I have a delightful inheritance." I know our society is *purpose driven* crazy these days, but the truth is, we each do have a purpose, a portion, a part to play in history that no one else can fill. Although there are similarities, we each have been assigned a cup to drink that's different from everyone else's. This scripture tells us that God has provided us with boundary lines to work within so we can focus on our proper assignment. We don't have to engage in a constant dilemma as to whether we are doing all we could or should be doing. But all too often, even as Christians, we don't recognize the freedom we have.

The predicament of discovering our *cup* has especially affected women in the last decades. My daughter (who recently graduated from law school) wears a t-shirt that sums it up well: "Be the lawyer your mother always wanted you to marry." Women are told that they can do everything a man can do *plus* be a wife and mother. The boundaries have been removed, but instead of freedom, many women struggle when faced with so many options. True freedom comes when we realize that being in God's will is all that really matters. I can be doing laundry, vacuuming, and changing diapers (hopefully not at the same time); I can be writing a book, teaching, and counseling; I can be caring for an elderly parent, working as a CEO, or running a political campaign. The important thing is to stay within the perimeters God has assigned. That's what gives meaning to even mundane tasks.

Not so with the culture of death, which says that since there are no inherent boundaries, we are free to determine our own limits in everything. The rule is no rules. No one voiced it more clearly than John Lennon in his song "Imagine" when he encouraged listeners to imagine there's no heaven, hell or religion. He envisioned a world where everyone would live for "today" resulting in complete peace and harmony. Sounds like freedom, but without limits, there can be no true freedom because everyone's freedom eventually conflicts with someone else's. Ironically, Lennon became the victim of his own philosophy when he was killed by someone who had no boundaries of right and wrong. We can counter this mentality when we realize that the boundaries God has provided fall in "pleasant places."

Psalm 16 continues with verse 7: "I will praise the Lord, who counsels me; even at night my heart instructs me." Another characteristic of our inheritance of life is that we have answers to problems—because the Lord counsels us. Isaiah called him the Wonderful "Counselor" (9:6). Jesus promised to send us a "Counselor" who would be with us forever, and that Counselor is the Spirit of truth (John 14:16 –17). We have the truth within us and that truth is the basis for solving every dilemma we face.

The culture of death doesn't have answers because it doesn't embrace truth. When we think our problems are too complicated for God to fix or when we despair because we don't have an immediate answer to a friend's crisis, it may be that we have been watching too much daytime TV. Psalm 16:7 says that God himself counsels us, even at *night* when we don't normally perceive anything—kind of like flying without visibility.

Pilots describe what it means to fly "in the soup." It's when the fog sets in and occludes all the tangible markers on the ground or the horizon that would normally guide them to their destination. When visibility is gone, they have to fly according to what the instruments say, not according to their perception, because their perception at that time can be dangerously misleading. What they think is happening becomes so hazy that even experienced pilots can be in a dive and not know it. Similarly, there may be times when we face dilemmas that make us feel like we're flying "in the soup." But a part of our inheritance is that we've been given the instruments to show us the way out of those spiritual fogs. The presence of the Counselor, the Spirit of truth, enables us to move through whatever problem we face and bring it to resolution.

The next verses (8–9) of Psalm 16 state, "I have set the Lord always before me. Because he is at my right hand, I will not be shaken... my body also will rest secure..." Insecurity seems to be a hallmark of this culture of death. Few of us are immune to it. But here, the psalmist gives the antidote. He says that because the Lord is at his right hand, he won't be shaken. Our security comes from being attached to someone bigger than ourselves. We resemble children who ask their parents,

"Will you go with me?" when they have to encounter a new situation. It's the connection to someone who is braver or stronger than we are that stills our anxiety.

As our country has moved further and further away from God, we have turned to other sources for security: personal appearance, success, power, relationships; there are and have been a plethora of substitutes. And what has been the result? An unprecedented increase in insecurity. The sources we've substituted for God are too small and too temporary to provide the sense of security we all crave. But if believers will start claiming their inheritance by setting the Lord—not some lesser god—always before them, true security will be evidenced.

Psalm 16:10 continues "…because you will not abandon me to the grave, nor will you let your Holy One see decay." Another characteristic of our inheritance is God's promise that we will never be abandoned, in life or in death. Fear of abandonment hangs over much of our society. And it's no wonder. Husbands abandon wives; wives abandon husbands; children are being abandoned by parents, if not physically, then emotionally; children are abandoning elderly parents; friends abandon friends; and the list goes on. We're afraid of being left alone. Yet scripture after scripture not only exhorts us not to fear, but also tells us why we shouldn't fear. Here are just a few of these scriptures:

- Psalm 27:1: "The Lord is my light and my salvation—whom shall I fear? The Lord is the stronghold of my life, of whom shall I be afraid?"
- Psalm 46:1–2: "God is our refuge and strength, an ever-present help in trouble. Therefore we will not fear…."
- Psalm 91:5, 9: "You will not fear…if you make the Most High your dwelling…."
- Isaiah 54:17 (emphasis mine): "no weapon forged against you will prevail, and you will refute every tongue that accuses you. *This is the heritage of the servants of the Lord*…."

We don't have to be afraid of being left alone. Even if we mess up, we are not instantly cut off. It won't happen in God's universe. We have all done acts that are punishable, but God offers forgiveness, redemption, and adoption into his family. We are not illegitimate children. Whether our parents wanted us or not, God wants us. I think of my cousin, Anna, who was adopted by Rick and Carla Reed. As a tiny infant, she was abandoned—left on the doorstep of an orphanage in China, where she was cared for until a family came and purchased her life. She's now a Reed. She's loved just as much as the Reeds' other two daughters, Jennie and Katy. She's going to receive the same inheritance as they do, and she never has to fear being abandoned again. Neither do we.

Strategies Against Us

Just as Israel had to fight for their inheritance, we also must fight to secure ours. There are many forces that try to entice us to throw away our heritage. If Esau was willing to sell his birthright for a bowl of soup, we would be foolish not to recognize our own vulnerability. Two forces particularly present in the culture of death are compromise and mediocrity—if not resisted, they will undermine our legacy and blur the mark of life.

Compromise

King Hezekiah was a man who refused to listen to the spin of the world, and he taught the people of Judah to do the same. He didn't compromise even when in desperate straits. We find the story in 2 Kings 18.

After capturing all the surrounding cities, the Assyrian army was headed for Jerusalem. Sennacherib, the king of Assyria, had sent his field commanders to convince Hezekiah to surrender. Speaking directly to the people, he tried to pit them against the king. "Do not listen to Hezekiah....Choose life and not death" (verses 31–32). He marketed a deal to them that was hard to refuse: if they would just give up the land of their inheritance, Assyria supposedly would provide them with something just as good. If they only surrendered, he said he'd take them to a place just as prosperous. Of course, he failed to mention what was written in the fine print—they'd be slaves! (And you thought *spin* was created by US politicians.)

I find it interesting that Israel was being told to *choose life*. Seven hundred years before this, Moses had given them an admonition before entering the land. He had said, "…Now *choose life* so that you and your children may live and that you may love the Lord your God, listen to his voice and hold fast to him. For the Lord is your life and he will give you many years in the land…." (Deuteronomy 30:19–20, emphasis mine). Life to Israel encompassed far more than breathing in and out. It was living in the land God had promised them and being in a covenant relationship with him. It recognized that living apart from God wasn't life at all, for he was their life.

Sennacherib used the words of God, but spun them to mean something totally different. Choosing life in Assyrian terms actually meant an invitation to death, because there Judah's identity as a nation and God's children would be lost. Essentially, they would be absorbed into the Assyrian culture. But neither Hezekiah nor the people fell for the trap. They held on to the truth, refusing to even engage in conversation with the enemy. Their resistance to compromise worked. God miraculously delivered them.

We're well aware of the kind of spin we are constantly subjected to in an attempt to make compromise more palatable. For compromise to be effective, it has to take a seed of the truth and twist it in a way that pacifies our conscience. So, partial birth abortions become "late term abortions"; promiscuity means being "sexually active"; pornography hides behind "freedom of speech." The attempt to retool marriage into something it was never meant to be infiltrates the media, courts, legislatures, and to our shame, even churches.

The early church fathers knew that to compromise biblical truths meant the demise of Christianity. When Polycarp was asked by the heretics of his day to affirm their legitimacy, he didn't play around in thinking: *If I give a little, maybe they will someday come around.* He responded to their requests boldly, "I recognize you as the first born of Satan." He was eventually martyred. Sometimes the truth will cost us friends, reputation, and perhaps, even our lives; but compromise costs far more.

Never, never, never compromise the truth. That is drinking directly from the well of the culture of death. Don't ever let yourself think that the end justifies the means. It never does. No matter how lofty the end, don't rationalize ignoble means to get there. As Solzhenitsyn resolved in his Nobel address, "Let the lie come into the world, even dominate the world, but not through me."

Mediocrity

The culture of death has a penchant for mediocrity. As stated before, we've become a society, as a whole, where nothing is worth a great deal of effort. And it's choking our land. Cultural critic Bill Bennett quotes Williams College Sociology professor Philip Kasinitz's observation that Americans have become the object of ridicule on many American campuses. When immigrant students criticize each other for getting lazy, they say, "You're becoming American." Kasinitz says, "Those who work the hardest to keep American culture at bay have the best chance of becoming American success stories."[10] The irony is heartbreaking.

King Jehoash was plagued with a similar mindset. In 2 Kings 13:14–19, the prophet Elisha was nearing death. When Jehoash went to see him, Elisha gave him some arrows and instructed him on what to do. "'Take the arrows…and strike the ground.' He struck it three times and stopped. The man of God was angry with him and said, 'You should have struck the ground five or six times; then you would have defeated Aram and completely destroyed it. But now you will defeat it only three times.'" Jehoash revealed that he lacked the zeal necessary to completely defeat his enemies. His moderate enthusiasm would result in moderate success.

The mark of life calls for wholehearted commitment—a principle echoed in Ecclesiastes 9:10, "Whatever your hand finds to do, do it with all your might…."

Jesus loved radicalness in his followers. Remember the woman who crawled on her hands and knees through dusty, dirty streets, just to touch the hem of his garment? (Luke 8:44). How about the man who wouldn't stop making a fool of himself in front of everyone, as he tirelessly petitioned with a loud voice, "Son of David, have mercy on me" (Luke 18:38). Or the woman who lived on the wrong side of the tracks; she pursued Jesus, swallowing what dignity she had left, to beg for crumbs from the master's table for the sake of her daughter

(Mark 7:28). We might think Jesus would disapprove of such behavior, but far from it. He rewarded such desperate displays.

Don't be afraid to be radically devoted to the one who is even more radically devoted to you. Such sold-out passion emanates life. The world is looking to see a people who live what they believe. I love how Francis Schaeffer phrased it. His last book, *The Great Evangelical Disaster,* was dedicated "to a new, young generation—and to those in the older generation—who will stand and be counted as radicals for truth and for Christ."[11] But if you chose to be uncompromising, passionate, and radical, be prepared to face forces that want you to look just like the world, a world that reflects neither vibrancy nor attractiveness, a world bent on diffusing the mark of life.

The Cost

Have you ever attended an inspiring conference where you are charged with emotion and determination to live for Jesus as never before, only to find yourself blowing it the next day? We sometimes end up more discouraged than before we went. I think of Peter's emotional declaration when Jesus told him he was going to be crucified. "Even if I have to die with you, I will never disown you" (Mark 14:31). He was in effect saying, "Give me Jesus or give me death." But we all know that within twenty-four hours Peter had denied Jesus three times.

Jesus knew that Peter was going to deny him, but he didn't get frustrated and order him to give back the keys to the kingdom. Jesus understood that Satan would come against Peter and try to "sift him like wheat" (Luke 22:31). Suffering was headed Peter's way, but Jesus didn't ask that it not come. Instead, he prayed that Peter's faith would not fail (verse 32). We know that God answered Jesus' prayers. In later years Peter encouraged other believers by helping them see that the suffering he had endured became the very means by which his faith grew. He who had once denied Christ was so transformed through his sufferings that he was indeed able to give his own life for Christ's sake. For Peter, the price was worth it.

What price must we pay to receive our inheritance? Every inheritance is preceded with death, in the natural as well as the spiritual. Spiritual death entails dying to self. As my friend, Diane, once prayed, "It's not just 'give me Jesus or give me death' but 'give me death to give me Jesus.'" Jesus said, "If anyone would come after me, he must deny himself, take up his cross daily and follow me. For whoever wants to save his life will lose it, but whoever loses his life for me will find it" (Luke 9:23–24). Jesus is speaking of self-denial. Self-denial finds no welcome mat in the culture of death. Francis Schaeffer wrote in *True Spirituality* that the order for us is the same as it was for Christ when he said he was going to be rejected, slain, and raised.[12] When we deny ourselves, we are going through rejection; when we take up the cross, we are being slain; and when we follow him, we are being raised. This is not a once and done process. If we are to experience true spirituality in our lives, there is no other way than to daily be rejected, slain, and raised in very practical ways.

The disruptions we experience in life, rather than detouring us toward destruction, offer us the greatest opportunities to deny ourselves, take up the cross, and follow him. Instead of lapsing into self-pity or worse, we can seize the occasion and let the disturbances form us into something far purer and far nobler than what we were before. That something enables us to reject the culture of death and be marked with the inheritance of life.

A True Story and Modern-Day Parable

Rasmus Midgett served in the Coast Guard at Cape Hatteras in the late 1890s and early 1900s. In August of 1899, Rasmus was on duty. His job was to patrol the beach, up and down, looking, listening, for any sign of distress. Sometime between three in the morning and sunrise, Rasmus heard cries coming from the ocean, and he spotted a stranded vessel that was breaking up from the tremendous force of the pounding waves. It turned out to be the wreckage of the ship *Priscilla*. Already the captain of the ship and his family had been washed overboard. But ten crewmen remained stranded, desperately clinging to what was left of the boat that was rapidly falling to pieces.

At that moment, Rasmus had to make a decision. He knew there wouldn't be enough time for him to go to the station for help, but he was only one man. What could he do against such impossible odds? He had no time to waste. As soon as the next breaker rolled in to shore, he raced into the water as the giant wave receded. He shouted instructions to the ten stranded men. They must have sensed he was their only hope, so they followed his directions.

The first of the crew climbed down a rope that was hanging on the side of the battered ship. Rasmus was able to grab him and drag him from the path of the next crashing breaker to deposit him on the beach. Rasmus made that trip seven times, bringing each man safely to shore. He must have been exhausted, but three men, who were too feeble and bruised to climb down the ropes, remained on the vessel. For Rasmus, there was no option but to rush back into the turbulent waters. He managed to pull himself up the side of the ship. Now taxed almost beyond human endurance, he lifted one of the men to his shoulders, slid down the rope, and battled his way to the shore. He secured the man and then dashed into the waters to rescue the second crewman. And finally, with one last burst of energy, Rasmus Midgett repeated the whole operation a third time. All ten members of the crew were saved because of his heroic efforts. His feat is unparalleled in the annals of lifesaving.[13]

Rasmus Midgett possessed a quality of courage that sprang from his not loving his life so much *as to shrink from death*. Although we may never rescue someone from literal pounding surf, we are surrounded by turbulent waters. People are drowning in this culture of death. Some are desperately holding on to pieces of a ship that is rapidly crumbling. There are fellow Christians who are experiencing difficulties that are shaking their foundations. They're "flying in the soup," and they need someone to direct them back to the instruments. The days are coming when we aren't going to have time to go back to the station for help. We'll have to recognize, like Rasmus, that the job is ours. Whether we meet that challenge to run into the crashing waves will depend on the choices we make today. Will we love not our lives so much as to shrink from death?

Cassie Bernell, one of the Christian teenagers who was martyred at Columbine High School in Colorado, was a person just like you and me. The day she was killed she had taken a quote to school to share with her friends. It was from Martin Luther King: "If a man hasn't found something he will die for, he isn't fit to live." [14]

Amen.

Bearing the mark of life requires a bigger vision than what we find within ourselves. Only as we set our eyes on something infinitely larger do we radiate life and see the place of honor we've inherited as God's children. And it is the mark of integrity that enables us to assume that role and grasp the vision.

DIGGING DEEPER

1. What do you see as at least part of the "portion and cup" God has assigned to you?
2. Can you identify some boundaries God has given you? Have they felt restrictive or "pleasant"?
3. Can you name a time when you felt like you were "flying in the soup"? What was the outcome?
4. When and how have you dealt with insecurities in your life?
5. Do you ever fear being left alone? How do you deal with that fear?
6. Where have you seen the forces of compromise and mediocrity threatening to steal your inheritance of life?
7. What are some areas you have had to die to in order to find life?
8. Where can you rescue someone from the culture of death by reflecting the mark of life?

THE HONOR ROLE
THE MARK OF INTEGRITY

Be thou my vision, O Lord of my heart; Naught be all else to me, save that Thou art. Thou my best thought, by day or by night, Waking or sleeping, Thy presence my light.

—Old Irish hymn

WHEN I WAS in college I received a substantial amount of money in scholarships and grants to go to school. It wasn't that I was so smart. I was just poor. In fact, I was probably one of the poorest to apply to the school. I remember being so afraid of losing my scholarships if my name wasn't on the honor roll that I disciplined myself and studied as hard as seemed humanly possible—because no scholarships meant no school. There's a principle that experience taught me. Landing in a position requiring academic excellence actually motivated me to live up to it. My diligence not only enabled me to keep my scholarships, but in the process, I *became* smarter. I essentially began to live out the standard I was seeking to attain.

We've been given a position of honor as children of God. But we don't always feel *honorable*, especially after we've had a bout of selfishness or anger or jealousy. But as C.S. Lewis notes, "Very often the only way to get a quality in reality is to start behaving as if you had it already." He says that "pretense leads to the real thing."[15] So you might say we have an *honor role* to play. The mark of integrity entails embracing that role—living in honorable ways whether we feel like it or not— in order to fulfill it.

First Samuel 2:30 says God will honor those who honor him. But how do we honor him? Timothy, in his desire to influence other believers, may have asked the same question. Paul encouraged him to "...set an example for the believers in speech, in life, in love, in faith, and in purity" (1 Timothy 4:12). These five areas encompass a wide range of human activity, and for each area, God sets a standard. It is in reaching for that bar in each area that we honor God. Playing the *honor role*, so to speak, will help us to *integrate* God's standards into how we live. And the mark of integrity it creates will fix our names on God's *honor roll.*

Speech

Because our words pack so much power, an ample number of scriptures direct us to God's standard in how we should speak. A few examples follow:

- 2 Timothy 2:23–24: "Don't have anything to do with foolish and stupid arguments, because you know they produce quarrels and the Lord's servant must not quarrel..."
- Proverbs 20:3: "It is to a man's honor to avoid strife, but every fool is quick to quarrel."
- Proverbs 17:19: "He who loves a quarrel loves sin...."

Even with these admonishments, it can be tempting to get embroiled in "foolish, stupid arguments" that turn into quarrels. Perhaps this is an issue for some more than others. Some of us think that if we can just explain our point of view more clearly, surely the other person will come around. As much as my experience has taught me otherwise, I have to confess that at times I still think this way. And not surprisingly, my children have "inherited" the same mindset. My daughter, Bethany, argued her way through law school at the University of Virginia, and from the time he was little, Josiah was able to craft compelling reasons for everything he wanted, from why he should stay up late to why he should be allowed to eat Golden Grahams (i.e., "they have more calcium than milk"). Josiah is the only kid I know who would type out his Christmas list and accompany each item with an argument as to why we should get it for him. One of my favorite requests was: "a miniature dachshund—cute, cuddliness, one of God's most beautiful creatures!"

There are few areas where the "argumentative spirit" rises up in me more than in political debates. When I was growing up, my family loved to argue politics. Everyone in the family was a southern Ohio Democrat, except for poor Grandma, who was an Eisenhower Republican. But even among the rest of us, the viewpoints varied greatly. Often we would get into heated differences, and at times, those arguments would drive a wedge, especially between my dad and me. As I began to grow in the Lord, I sensed the Holy Spirit convicting me about arguing politics because of the separation it caused. I recognized how I would become more concerned with winning the argument than representing Christ's love. This isn't to say that it's wrong to argue issues, but there's a point in a discussion when it turns into a "quarrel," and for me, once it got to that place, there was no turning back.

A few years ago our friend Scott Boyd ran for State Representative. I dearly love Scott and his wife, Nancy; I knew he would make a great congressman. I wanted to do whatever I could to support him, but I knew I had to be careful not to "cross the line." On election day, my job consisted of going to the poll and handing out Boyd literature as people came to vote. When I arrived at the poll, a man representing Scott's chief opponent was already there. Because I thought Scott had been treated somewhat unfairly during the campaign, it wasn't long before that old familiar wall began to build. I made up my mind I didn't like him.

In the course of the morning we were joined by another volunteer, Sean, who was campaigning for yet a third candidate. As we began to chat, Sean described himself as "part Jewish, part atheist." Well, it wasn't long before the first man began talking to Sean about God's love. But I was stuck in a very *unloving* attitude! He was my opponent. This was war, not a love fest! I had to decide whether I would continue to shut him out or join with him in trying to bring a lost sheep to Christ. Thankfully, the higher call trumped my resistance, and all the separation I'd felt began to dissolve. By the end of the day, the self-professed atheist asked if he could call my husband and me to pursue spiritual questions. I had honored God by resisting the urge to argue, and as a result, Christ's love prevailed. (Incidentally, Scott won the election without my having to defend him).

Another way we honor God with our speech is through choosing not to complain or grumble. Philippians 2:14–15 says, "Do everything without complaining or arguing, so that you may become blameless and pure, children of God without fault...." This presents a clear indication of how what we say affects who we are. We become *blameless and pure* through not complaining. And this honors God. Have you ever noticed that the more we complain about something, the worse it becomes? That's because what we focus on tends to grow. Rather than complaining about a person or situation, we really do have the option to look for the good. And the more gratefulness we express, the more God is honored. I love the story Brennan Manning includes in his book *Ruthless Trust*:

> She had some kind of "wasting disease," her different powers fading away over the march of the month. A student of mine happened upon her on a coincidental visit. The student kept going back, drawn by the strange force of the woman's joy. Though she could no longer move her arms and legs, she would say, "I'm just so happy I can move my neck." When she could no longer move her neck, she would say, "I'm just so glad I can hear and see." When the young student finally asked the old woman what would happen if she lost her sound and sight, the gentle old lady said, "I'll just be so grateful that you come to visit."[16]

There are many things in life that we have no control over, but as this incident so powerfully illustrates, we *can chose* not to be negative. As we choose to honor the Lord with our mouths, our speech more and more will reveal the mark of integrity.

Life

If we are to honor God in life, to quote Francis Schaeffer's perceptive book, "How should we then live?" In four words... *not like the world*.

Author David Wells defines worldliness as "a system of values which has at its center our human perspective, and makes sin look normal and righteousness seem strange."[17] If this definition of worldliness is correct, it doesn't take a great deal of insight to realize how inundated we are with "sin looking normal and righteousness seeming strange." From TV sitcoms to movies to magazines to advertisements...*sin looks normal*. This is a drastic change, even from a few years ago. When I was growing up, TV shows were so different than those of today. My favorite was *Father Knows Best*. There was always a moral to be learned about taking responsibility or being honest or caring for each other. Righteous behavior didn't seem odd. Compare that with "lessons" we can learn from the present fare of *Desperate Housewives, Wife Swap,* and *The Simpsons*. It used to be that the indiscretions of the "rich and famous" rarely made headlines, but if news of immoral behavior did surface, it would be roundly criticized. Today, a celebrity gets pregnant, and everyone tries to *guess* the father's identity, and it's not considered abnormal.

Worldliness embraces a mindset where self-interest triumphs over duty and self-gratification over responsibility. Rather than rejecting this way of thinking, David Wells points out that the baby boomers, who now comprise over half the church, brought this perspective with them when they joined. He says that Christianity offered them a deal they couldn't refuse. For a one-time admission of weakness and failure, they got eternal peace with God. They took the deal and went on with their lives as before. The result has been that there is no significant difference between the lifestyle of many "born-again Christians" and that of non-believers. It's as if the Westminster Confession got hijacked from "the chief end of man is to love God and enjoy him forever" to "love yourself and indulge forever."

One of the most devastating consequences of this self-focus and independence is a sense of disconnectedness from everything around us. We think that what we do doesn't really affect anyone else. We abandon any consciousness of moral responsibility to whatever group we may belong—family, business, church. For example, when people used to commit a dishonorable act, there was an understanding that it naturally reflected on their family. My friend Jen shared how her father used to say to her before she went out, "Remember you're a VanHeel." There was an acknowledgement that how she conducted herself would reflect on the family name. That sense is being lost. Look at the workplace. A recent poll reported that only 19% of employees responded they were in their job "for the long haul." When is the last time you interacted with an employee who you felt cared about his or her company's reputation? I was in a store the other day and two different employees suggested two other stores for me to find what I was looking for—even though their store had the items!

Even more important than the disconnectedness from everything around us, we stand in great danger of thinking in such individualistic terms that we forget we really do represent the Lord. Billy Graham once said that his greatest fear was that he might do something or say something that would bring disrepute on the gospel of Christ. His ministry has reflected the integrity of that mindset. He understands that how we act in situations has implications that can bring either honor or dishonor to God.

For example, our diligence—or lack thereof—in our work reflects on God. I saw this one summer when Bethany worked as a hostess in a restaurant. Her job offered low pay, high disorganization, and a constant turnover of employees. But she stuck it out. One evening when Chip and I went in for dinner, we were talking with one of the servers who commented on how he loved it when Bethany worked because she displayed such a good work ethic—a rarity, he said. She brought honor to God (and her family) just by doing her duty.

The standard we are to live by is the antithesis of the worldly perspective. Philippians 2:3–4 says, "Do nothing out of selfish ambition or vain conceit, but in humility consider others better than yourselves. Each of you should look not only to your own interests, but also to the interests of others." Living *not like the world* checks our egocentric thinking and enables us to give honor to the One to whom it is truly due.

Love

The standard of love that honors God is love that loves like he does. Jesus said we are to love one another *as he has loved us*. And *he has loved us* the way the Father has loved him. Jesus said in John 15:9, "As the Father has loved me, so have I loved you. Now remain in my love." Jesus' love was rooted and sustained through obedience to the Father. And through our responsiveness to him, ours will be as well. That means our love is not dependent upon others' receptivity. They may reject us in return. They may be unlovable. They may be disinterested. They may have nothing to give back. But through Christ, we can love them anyway.

It was this kind of love that enabled Paul to care so deeply for his spiritual children. When the church in Corinth began resisting his authority, he didn't give up in exasperation or withhold his affection. He appealed to them, "I will very gladly spend for you everything I have and expend myself as well. If I love you more, will you love me less? Be that as it may..." (2 Corinthians 12:15–16). In essence, he's saying, "If you don't love me in return, so what? My love for Christ compels me to carry out the call he has given me to love you." Because Paul doesn't need their approval, he can love them freely, without expectation. This is the kind of love we are to emulate if we want to honor God. When we face people who are hard to love, our devotion to Christ can catapult us to a greater depth of love, for *his* sake.

My friend Joanne had a husband who suffered with a chronic illness for over nine years. Gary's condition slowly deteriorated until it reached the point where he was no longer able to work; he tired easily, and he had to fight periodic bouts of depression due to his medication. Sometimes the burden of caring for Gary and their two teenage daughters, along with holding a full-time teaching position, overwhelmed Joanne. On occasion she felt like all she was doing was giving, giving, giving, with little in return. Her paradigm shifted, however, when she heard a speaker exhort believers to give *everything* to the Lord. As an example he said, "What if the Lord sent you to an island, where your whole ministry was to help one leper?" Joanne began thinking about her husband, and it struck her that perhaps caring for him was the most important thing God had asked her to do in life. Gary had no family other than her and their girls. Who else would intercede for him like her? Who else would take the time to make sure he ate healthy food? Who else would have the patience and endurance to see him through the times of despondency? Who else would cry out to God for grace on his behalf? Her whole perspective began to change as she felt herself rise to the challenge of sacrificial love for the Lord's sake. Although she dearly loved her husband, it was her love for God and obedient response to his call that propelled her to a new dimension of God-honoring love.

As we follow the command to love each other as Christ has loved us, the mark of integrity it displays will bring great honor to God. "This is to my Father's glory [honor] that you bear much fruit, showing yourselves to be my disciples" (John 15:8).

Faith

"…though now for a little while you may have had to suffer grief in all kinds of trials. These have come so that your faith—of greater worth than gold, which perishes even though refined by fire—may be proved genuine and may result in praise, glory and *honor* when Jesus Christ is revealed" (1 Peter 1:6–7 emphasis mine). Faith refined by fire is faith that honors God. When we continue to trust God in spite of the difficulties we face, when we tenaciously hold on in hope to the promises he has given, when we refuse to let our trials make us doubt his love for us, we are honoring God through our faith. This is where Moses, although a great man of God, failed. It's recoded in Numbers 20.

Moses and Aaron had led the Israelites in the dessert for forty years. Finally, what they had longed for was about to be fulfilled. They would be saying good-bye to manna, quail, and endless dessert sand. Four decades of literally walking in circles was about to come to an end. They were going to enter the Promised Land. And no one could have been anticipating it more than Moses. But there was a problem. Once again they had run out of water, and the people started complaining and grumbling. They were so disgruntled that they proclaimed they would rather die than go on! In spite of such an incredulous statement, Moses interceded on their behalf. God graciously answered by instructing Moses to speak to a rock; as he did, water would pour forth.

However, the people's complaints were too much for Moses. He'd had enough. Hadn't those rebels learned anything in forty years? Filled with frustration, Moses took the situation into his own hands. Angrily, he took his staff and *struck* the rock, rather than speak to it as God had commanded. God faithfully made water pour forth, but he was not pleased with how Moses misrepresented his holiness to the people. He said to Moses, "Because you did not trust me enough to honor me as holy in the sight of the Israelites, you will not bring this community into the land I give them" (Numbers 20:12). Moses had allowed his own weakness to color his perception of God. He didn't honor God enough to trust him to do what he said he would do. His faith had faltered, causing God's holiness to be tarnished.

A famous study was conducted in the 60s at the University of Pennsylvania. Dogs were given random electric shocks over which they had no control. No matter what they did, they couldn't stop the shocks. Later, they were put in a situation where they could easily stop them—all they had to do was step over a barrier. Usually, dogs quickly learn to do this, but not these dogs. They had *learned* they were powerless to stop the shocks. So they didn't even try. Their reaction was termed "learned helplessness."[18] It's the giving up reaction, the quitting response that follows the belief that whatever one does, it doesn't matter.

Some of us are like those dogs. Because of past wounds, we've set up invisible fences around our hearts. We're conditioned to believe that it really doesn't matter whether we trust God or not— we're going to get shocked anyway, and we don't want the pain. Nevertheless, to continue to have faith in God, even when it seems there is no hope, brings honor to him. If we dare to keep trusting, those very moments of despair will forge in us the mark of integrity. Brennan Manning puts it this way:

> Often trust begins on the far side of despair. When all human resources are exhausted, when the craving for reassurances is stifled, when we forego control, when we cease trying to manipulate God and demystify Mystery, then—at our wits' end—trust happens within us, and the untainted cry, "Abba, into your hands I commend my spirit," surges from the heart.[19]

We may never know what could have been accomplished through us or how greatly God might have been honored had we but trusted. Dr. Henrietta Mears, founder of Gospel Light Publications, and considered by many to have had the most far-reaching impact on Christian ministry of any woman in the twentieth century, is reported to have made an interesting commentary on her deathbed. When asked if she would do anything differently if she could do it over again, she thoughtfully replied, "If I had it to do over again, I would have trusted Christ more."[20] What a profound assessment from one used so greatly. Let's not get to our deathbeds and regret that we didn't trust Christ more. Whether in the great trials of life or in the challenges of everyday obedience, let's not be risk-free Christians. Let's embrace the mark of integrity and dare to honor God with our faith.

Purity

The final area Paul mentions in which we can honor God is purity. "In a large house there are articles not only of gold and silver, but also of wood and clay; some are for noble purposes and some for ignoble. If a man cleanses himself from the latter, he will be an instrument for noble purposes, made holy, useful to the Master and prepared to do any good work" (2 Timothy 2:20–21). How do we go about cleansing ourselves for higher purposes? Maybe an easier question to answer would be: What keeps us from it? Apathy? Laziness? Are we just plain comfortable being a wooden or clay vessel, or is there something deeper at play? Do we really believe that God has called us to be vessels of gold and silver, created for noble, honorable works?

I believe that if we are to honor God in purity, we must first be cleansed from an underlying sense of shame. Our shame directs us to focus on our flaws and weaknesses, and as we do, we become even less useful, causing yet more shame. We think God never could answer *our* prayers of intercession, so we don't pray. We think God never could use *our* testimony to bring someone into the kingdom, so we don't witness. We think *we* never could hear God tell us to do something radical, so we don't listen. And we are woefully ashamed of our barrenness.

We don't talk a lot about shame, even though much of our culture is driven by it. I think it's because we're too ashamed to admit we're ashamed. But most of us experience it. Shame always reflects a feeling of unacceptability. In some way, we feel we haven't measured up to a particular standard. We're not successful enough, rich enough, spiritual enough, or maybe we just have bad hair. How many people skip class reunions because they're ashamed of the weight they've gained? We feel ashamed for the wrong reasons.

On the other hand, when we've sinned, we should feel shame. Then it's tied to guilt *for something we've done*, not to who we are. We get rid of that kind of shame through repentance. But the other kind of shame sticks like glue. It's hard to get rid of because it comes as a result of attaching ourselves to the wrong standards. The answer to shame is acceptance, but the only acceptance deep enough to tear us away from our shame is the acceptance that comes from God. Psalm 25:3 tells us that those who hope in the Lord will never be put to shame because hope in him is the right standard.

Hope of being in and like Christ actually begins the purifying process in us, not only because it gives us the right standard, but also because it causes a change in us. First John 3:2–3 says, "…now we are children of God, and what we will be has not yet been made known. But we know that when he appears, we shall be like him, for we shall see him as he is. Everyone who has this hope in him purifies himself, just as he is pure." In shifting the focus from our inadequacy to Jesus' adequacy, our insufficiency to his sufficiency, we become more like the object of our focus, and we literally are transformed. We begin to understand that Christ is not focused on our shortcomings—so why should we be? Remember when he called Peter the "rock" in Matthew 16:18? Jesus obviously perceived how wavering and unsteady Peter was, but he was able to see beyond his flaws. Jesus will do the same for us. Our unworthiness has nothing to do with our destiny in Christ. We will never somehow manage to get "good enough" to be worthy of his honor. We are worthy because his love deems us so. And the cross proves it.

We don't have to be on the front lines of battle to attain the mark of integrity. We don't have to be a statesman, missionary, or marine. We don't have to be perfect. All we have to be is a child of God, exhibiting the role of honor we are called to live. As we fix our eyes on the standard he has set and integrate it into our speech, life, love, faith, and purity, we will leave behind a far richer heritage than we could have ever imagined. As he becomes our *vision*, our "best thought by day or by night," we will find the path higher than we would have chosen for ourselves—but more attainable and lasting than all our lesser goals…

> Riches I heed not, nor man's empty praise,
> Thou my inheritance, now and always,
> Thou and Thou only, first in my heart,
> High King of Heaven, my treasure Thou art. [21]

As that vision of God is sealed in our hearts, we find a new strength to fight the battles we face. The mark of integrity inevitably leads to a mark sought in as many circumstances as there are people—the mark of victory.

DIGGING DEEPER

1. How do you know when a discussion has turned into a "quarrel"?
2. What can you do to resist falling into "foolish, stupid arguments"?
3. Do you consider yourself more of a complainer or more of one who looks for the good in situations?
4. How do you fight the pull of self-interest and self-gratification over duty and responsibility?
5. Where have you experienced love without expectations (either as the recipient or the giver)?
6. Have you ever gone through situations of "learned helplessness"? How have you pushed through?
7. Are there any areas of shame that have affected your life? How can you find freedom?
8. As you look over the five areas discussed in this chapter, which ones need to be more integrated into your life?

CHAPTER 6

MORE THAN CONQUERORS
THE MARK OF VICTORY

Yet we have this consolation with us, that the harder the conflict, the more glorious the triumph. What we obtain too cheap, we esteem too lightly; it is dearness only that gives everything its value.
—Thomas Paine
The Crises

I'M NOT A big pro football fan, but the 2006 NFL playoffs caught my attention. The Pittsburgh Steelers were playing against the favored Indianapolis Colts in the AFC semifinals. It was a big game; the winner would advance one step closer to the Super Bowl. The Steelers were ahead 21 to 18, with 1:27 remaining on the clock. They had the ball on the two yard line. The Pittsburgh coach wanted to run out the time, so he called for a pitch to running back Jerome Bettis. Bettis, who was set to retire at the end of the season, had touched the ball 3,695 times in his career and only fumbled on forty-one plays. Unfortunately, this would be number forty-two. As he was hit, the ball popped loose and was quickly picked up by the Colts' cornerback, who ran *untouched* for thirty yards. Quarterbacks rarely tackle, but in this case, a touchdown was prevented when Steelers' quarterback, Ben Roethlisberger, was finally able to bring him down. The Colts worked their way to field goal range with only seventeen seconds left in the game. Colts' Mike Vanderjagt was the most accurate field goal kicker in the NFL. He was set to kick for three points, tie the game, and go into overtime. But in what had already been a series of unusual events, Vanderjagt kicked to the right and missed! The Steelers won. What had looked like victory, then defeat, finally resulted in the big win.

I relate this story not because I think the Lord devised a plan for the Steelers to prevail, but because it reminds me of how much God wants us to win. Even when we are down to the finish line and fumble the ball, he is able to orchestrate success in the most unusual ways. He has marked us for victory.

God intends for each of us to be "more than conquerors." Romans 8:37 says, "...in all these things we are more than *conquerors* through him who loved us" (emphasis mine). Synonyms for conquer include vanquish, defeat, beat, lick, subdue, reduce, overcome, overthrow, and rout—an apt description of the mindset we are to cultivate if we want to be true conquerors. The latter part of the verse reveals how we are to accomplish this feat: "through him who loved us." Only by staying connected to his love will we experience the mark of victory, because it is through his love that we win. A closer look at this passage from Romans reveals the what, the why, and the how of bearing that mark and becoming *more than a conqueror*.

The What

What needs to be conquered? Romans 8:35 lists some of the things that potentially separate us from God's love and keep us from victory. "Who shall separate us from the love of Christ? Shall trouble or hardship or persecution or famine or nakedness or danger or sword?" How about screaming children or cancer or unmet expectations or personal rejection or busted car windows or unanticipated bills? How about all of the above? Even though the scripture says these things cannot separate us from his love, we know that when circumstances like these occur, we can *feel* like God doesn't care about us. In verses 38–39, Paul reiterates that *nothing* can separate us from the love of God: "...neither death, nor life, neither angels nor demons, neither the present nor the future, nor any powers, neither height nor depth nor anything else in all creation, will be able to separate us from the love of God that is in Christ Jesus our Lord." Nothing exists or will exist that extends beyond the reach of a loving God.

Although many situations such as these may threaten our confidence, a few pose particularly strong challenges.

Betrayal and Rejection

Betrayal and rejection can crush our confidence and completely upend the mark of victory. Betrayal comes in many forms. Wives or husbands who have been betrayed by spouses find it very hard to trust anyone again, including God. Those who have been molested and abused as children have great difficulty recognizing a God who loves them and who will not use his authority to exploit them. I know a woman whose alcoholic father said terrible, rejecting things to her when he had been drinking. Even though she knew better than to believe his spiteful remarks, his cruelty tainted her perception of God as a loving Father. "If an enemy were insulting me, I could endure it; if a foe were raising himself against me, I could hide from him. But it is you, a man like myself, my companion, my close friend," laments the psalmist (Psalm 55:12–13). We may be able to withstand an enemy or stranger rejecting us, but when it comes to someone who is or should be a confidant, we are shaken to the core. If our sense of worth stems from "significant others," as it often does, it's hard not to think something is wrong with us when they reject us. It is at this point that we can either accuse God of being unfair, or embrace his love to bring us through.

All too often we attribute unfairness in life to God. But life in this world has been distorted from its original intent. C. S. Lewis refers to humans as being "bent" due to the consequences of the fall. We all have "bent" sin natures that can hurt other people. Our free will can choose good or evil, and God typically won't override our choice in order to fix things. So in a fallen world, our hope can never be that rejection and betrayal won't happen. We have the assurance, however, that the rejections and betrayals we experience will be used, in time, for our ultimate good (Romans 8:28).

Jesus knows all about our suffering. He was "despised and rejected by men" (Isaiah 53:3) as no one else has ever been. All of his disciples deserted him at Gethsemane. One of his twelve betrayed him, and the one on whom he would build his church denied him three times. But the rejection and betrayal he suffered resulted in the greatest good known to mankind. The mark of victory was etched deeper than his wounds—in fact, *because of his wounds.* And so it is with us.

Rejection and betrayal do not have to separate us from God's love. In fact, they can be the very instruments God uses to redemptively draw us near and position us for the true riches. Brennan Manning, in challenging believers to look beyond suffering and to relentlessly remain confident in the character of Christ no matter what we face, puts it eloquently: "The splendor of a human heart that trusts it is unconditionally loved gives God more pleasure and causes him more delight than the most magnificent cathedral ever erected or the most thunderous organ ever played."[22]

Failure

Sometimes we think that if we are in God's will we should never experience failure. When we have sunk our best efforts, time, and resources into a project only to come up empty, we can feel that God is not for us. It seems like the mark of defeat, not victory, characterizes our lives. So we begin to withdraw and allow our discouragement to keep God at arm's length. But like betrayal and rejection, failure is part of life in a fallen world. And like betrayal and rejection, it is also redeemable.

There are few people who have achieved success in life who have not first gone through a baptism of failure. Politicians, athletes, and business executives; authors, entertainers, and inventors; farmers, artists, and generals—we all fail. Sometimes it's the failure that teaches us how to live with the success. Or failure might be necessary for the completion of God's bigger plan. Such was the case with Robert E. Lee.

We all know Lee commanded the Confederate army during the Civil War. What is less known, however, is the fact that he hated slavery and vehemently opposed the South's secession from the Union. But to fight with the North would have caused him to turn against all his family and friends in Virginia. Because of his loyalty to them, he went with the South. Lee is considered to be the greatest military genius of his century and one of the greatest in all history. Yet, he lost the Civil War, and the battle he is remembered most for is Gettysburg, a crushing defeat for his army, the turning point of the whole war. A deeply committed Christian, Lee took full responsibility for the loss. He had prepared and had relied on God for the battle, but the victory was not to be.

A testimony to Lee's greatness lay in his ability to handle both success and failure. Even after the war when he was stripped of his American citizenship, he never became embittered. He constantly exhorted the South to be reconciled to the North. A key to his attitude was a profound awareness of his own sin. He once wrote, "Man's nature is so selfish. So weak. Every feeling, every passion urging him to follow excess and sin [so] that I am disgusted with myself and sometimes with all the world."[23] He recognized the depth of love it took for God to forgive him, and his gratitude compelled him to want the will of God more than anything else, even if it meant his failure. It's been reported that after the battle of Gettysburg, a revival broke out in the Southern army, and 15,000 men were converted to Christ. Who knows but that their defeat positioned them for salvation and *eternal* victory?

If you have questioned whether or not God is for you because you have met circumstances with less "success" than you wanted, don't let the failure keep you distant from God. I've often heard it said that God reproves us more for failing to try than trying and failing. "God is not unjust; he will not forget your work and the love you have shown him as you have helped his people and continue to help them" (Hebrews 6:10).

Overlooking the Small Stuff

Another area that can result in separation from God is found in our tendency to overlook the small, seemingly insignificant issues that put subtle wedges between us and God. Distractions that keep us too busy to read the Bible and spend time in prayer may seem like they're not taking a toll, but they can cause us to forget the intimacy we once enjoyed. Resistance to the leading of the Holy Spirit in little acts of obedience can eventually move to blatant demonstrations of putting our own agenda above God's. Refusal to repent when convicted causes our hearts to harden bit by bit. We may not recognize the impact these areas of neglect have on our spiritual life until we find ourselves in the throes of defeat and wonder why.

It's similar to the "broken window" theory. A number of large cities have reduced the rate of serious crimes like murder, drug dealing, and robbery by first attending to minor areas of crime like loitering, panhandling, and graffiti. Coined the "broken window theory," it stems from the observation that if a broken window in a building is left unrepaired, soon all the windows are knocked out. Neglect of the *small stuff* sent the message that no one cared, a message which actually invited further vandalism. In the early 1990s when this theory was first put into practice, New York City's most dangerous precinct went from 129 to 47 homicides in a three-year period. Although some critics attribute the decline to other factors, most researchers agree that some connection exits between minor and major offenses.

The principle that minor areas should not be overlooked can be extended to our lives. God generously gives us broken windows to fix in order to train and prepare us for the bigger issues that we are called to conquer.

The Why

God desires for us to be more than conquerors because he loves us so deeply. We've gotten so accustomed to framing God's love in trite phrases that we've lost a sense of the strength of what he feels for us. Two of the most forceful images he uses in the Old Testament to communicate his love can be found in the strongest human bonds we experience: that of a husband and wife, and that of a parent and child.

Husband and Wife

Most biblical scholars concur that the Song of Solomon not only depicts the relationship between Solomon and his bride, but also allegorizes the relationship between Christ and his bride, the church. Expositor J. Sidlow Baxter comments, "The writing has an historical basis; but in harmony with the rest of Scripture, it also has a religious purpose and a spiritual content. An ideal human love is represented, to lead the soul into the thought of fellowship with God."[24]

Throughout the Song of Solomon we find vivid descriptions of God's love likened to that of a husband for his wife. Overwhelmed with her beauty, he declares, "You have stolen my heart, my sister, my bride; you have stolen my heart…" (4:9). The King James translates "stolen" as "ravished." Imagine that.God loves you so much that you *ravish* his heart. When the bride goes through trials and difficulties, yet remains loyal to him, he responds, "Turn your eyes from me; they overwhelm me" (6:5). One author comments how God is not overcome with armies or sunsets or angels; he's overwhelmed with irresistible love as he sees her faithful devotion.[25] The strength of his love is captured in 8:7, "Many waters cannot quench love; rivers cannot wash it away. If one were to give all the wealth of his house for love, it would be utterly scorned."

Other passages in Scripture reveal the steadfast nature of God's love, even when it is spurned. After Israel rebelled and started worshiping other gods, the Lord spoke through the prophet Jeremiah, "'Return faithless people,' declares the Lord, 'for I am your husband'" (Jeremiah 3:14). Her brazen unfaithfulness is depicted in the following verses. "Long ago you broke off your yoke and tore off your bonds; you said, 'I will not serve you!' Indeed, on every high hill and under every spreading tree you lay down as a prostitute" (Jeremiah 2:20). "…you said, 'It's no use! I love foreign gods, and I must go after them'" (Jeremiah 2:25). Yet even such shamelessness as this does not kill his love. "I have loved you with an everlasting love; I have drawn you with loving-kindness. I will build you up again and you will be rebuilt, O *Virgin Israel…*" (31:3–4, emphasis mine). God saw beyond her spiritual apostasy as if it never happened. In his eyes, the *prostitute* becomes the *virgin*. What a picture of redemptive love! This is a redemptive love that is offered to us as well. It is not quenched by our doubts, rebellion, or unfaithfulness. He loves us as a loyal, faithful husband.

Parent and Child

The second major way God illustrates his love for us is through the image of a parent and child. Most parents who have had children in sports understand how love wants to see their children win. I remember one time when Josiah was playing football. As he carried the ball into the end zone, I practically ran down the sidelines with him! It's hard for me to imagine anyone beaming more than parents when their children stand in the winner's circle. Yet God rejoices even more in the victories of his children.

Still, his love remains steadfast whether we win or lose, and even when we rebel against him. "Is not Ephraim my dear son, the child in whom I delight? Though I often speak against him, I still remember him. Therefore my heart yearns for him; I have great compassion for him" (Jeremiah 31:20). "How long will you wander, O unfaithful daughter?" (Jeremiah 31:22). Despite Israel's rejection, God didn't stop reaching out his hand. "How gladly would I treat you like sons and give you a desirable land, the most beautiful inheritance of any nation. I thought you would call me 'Father' and not turn away from following me" (Jeremiah 3:19). Do you hear the heartbreak expressed in that verse? Not only were they refusing to acknowledge God as their Father, they were even calling "wood" and "stone" their father and mother, indicating how far they had fallen into idolatry (Jeremiah 2:27).

God relentlessly extended his love to Israel, just as he does to us. As strong as an earthly father or mother's love may be for his or her child, God's love is stronger. God will find ways to reveal love to his children to the very end.

I saw this loving pursuit in the life of Sarah Lowry. Sarah was raised in a strict Mennonite home. A quiet woman, she obtained her nursing degree and served as a missionary in Belize for two years. Although she had attended church all her life, she had a hard time matching up what she knew in her head about God with what she felt in her heart. She eventually married, and she and her husband Grant began attending our church. But her inability to experience God's love continued to plague her. When we announced an upcoming ladies' conference, Sarah decided to come. I will never forget walking down the hall with her at the end of the weekend. I asked her how her time had been. She said for the first time in her life she felt the connection between her heart and head in God's love for her. After all those years, she was finally free.

Two weeks later, Sarah died unexpectedly. I don't understand why Sarah suffered some of the things she did in her life, or why it took her so long to experience God's love. But I do know that her heavenly Father unremittingly pursued her to the end. It was as if he was saying, "Here, daughter, let me help you finish your race."

The How

God teaches us how to be more than conquerors by putting us in situations where we *have* to overcome. Can I say that again? God teaches us how to be more than conquerors by putting us in situations where we *have* to overcome. The very obstacles that would hinder us become the opportunities that instruct us. C. S. Lewis illustrates this well in *The Horse and His Boy*. It's a story about a boy and his talking horse who escape from their evil owners to Narnia. In their travels, they learn that another country is going to invade Narnia and they must get there in time to warn the king. Along the trip they are hounded by wild animals and forced to swim for their lives. They trudge through deserts, where they almost die of heat and thirst. Then, when they are just about to reach their goal, a lion chases them, causing them to use every last ounce of strength they have to make it to safety.

After this, the boy meets Aslan and complains to him, saying how he must be the unluckiest boy in the world, as he relates all the things that had befallen him. Aslan responds, "I do not call you unfortunate…I was the lion who forced you to go on…I was the lion who gave the Horses the new strength of fear for the last mile so that you should reach King Lune in time."[26] Had it not been for the obstacles, the boy never would have pushed himself beyond what he thought he was capable of doing.

Has God ever allowed "lions" to come your way to help you learn how to push through to new victories? The Bible is replete with examples for us to follow, but Joshua, Nehemiah, and Paul stand out as three who especially faced their share of lions. They serve as models of those who faced obstacles, embraced them, and as a result, became conquerors.

Joshua assisted Moses in leading Israel in the desert for forty years before they were allowed to enter the Promised Land. It was the obstacles the nation faced during that time that prepared them for the insurmountable odds they would come up against once they began taking the land. Forty years before, their unbelief had prevented them from entering. Now they were a changed people; the wilderness had purged them of their self-reliance and lack of faith. They had learned that everything they needed—from the water they drank, to the food they ate, to the long-lasting shoes they wore—was supplied by the Lord. So they were ready to defeat their enemies in the way God directed. They could march around the walls of Jericho seven times, blow their trumpets, shout, and watch the walls implode (see Joshua 7). They could enter into battles— outnumbered—and watch God hurl hailstones and cause the sun to stop until their success was complete (Joshua 10:1-14). Joshua led them to victory against the Amorites, Canaanites, Hittites, Perizzites, Jebusites, and Hivites. Even when the enemies joined forces, they could not prevail against Israel (Joshua 21:44).

Nehemiah also faced what appeared to be an impossible task. He was sent to rebuild the walls of Jerusalem. The city had been destroyed by Babylon and had lain in ruins for 140 years. The walls were broken, the gates burned, and those who had returned from exile had gotten used to it. But it was disgraceful for the people to live in such a vulnerable state with no way of protecting themselves. It was a visible symbol that they were not *more than conquerors*; they were the *conquered*. Nehemiah met obstacles almost immediately in his task. When the wall was rebuilt to half its height, the enemies plotted to kill the workers. But undaunted, Nehemiah persisted, and the people worked with a sword in one hand and a trowel in the other. False reports were sent to the king in another maneuver to halt the work, but Nehemiah refused to be intimidated, and finally the work was finished. "So the wall was completed…in fifty-two days" (Nehemiah 6:15). That's incredible! A 140-year symbol of defeat wiped out in fifty-two days!

Paul faced obstacles from the moment he started preaching. In one way or another he was forced to leave almost every city he visited: Iconium, Lystra, Phillipi, Thessalonica, Berea, Ephesus, and Jerusalem. In 2 Corinthians 11:23–28, we find a litany of the forces arrayed against him. He had been imprisoned more frequently and flogged more severely than anyone. He'd been beaten, stoned, shipwrecked, and left for dead. He encountered danger from rivers, bandits, Jews, and Gentiles. He experienced sleepless nights, an empty stomach, and exposure to the cold. Plus, he bore a constant burden for the welfare of the believers.

But despite the challenges, he laid the foundation for the church, a foundation which has lasted over 2,000 years.

Obstacles will always come to hinder the work of God. Some of us may have to face, as did Joshua and the Israelites, a confrontation with our self-reliance and unbelief. Some of us have broken walls in our lives that make us vulnerable to the enemy. Every time we've tried to rebuild, a shadow of defeat has covered our minds, causing us to buy into the lie that our "burnt stones can't live again" (see Nehemiah 4:2).Or maybe we can relate to some of the difficulties Paul faced—physical abuse and deprivation for the sake of the truth, slander from false brothers, pressure of concern for those in the church. Yet Joshua, Nehemiah, and Paul stood firm against overwhelming odds. And so can we.

What caused these men to be more than conquerors? I believe three commonalities marked them with victory. First, they each had clarity in their call. When things got tough, they didn't vacillate as to whether or not they were in the will of God. They *knew* they were. Second, they exhibited total reliance on God rather than themselves. They possessed a keen awareness that the only way they could succeed was if God was in control. They manifested a humble dependence on his game plan. Third, these men displayed a deep reverence for the Word of God. They understood that his word was the most important weapon in their arsenal, and they refused to take it lightly. We hear them stressing the significance of God's Word as they neared the completion of their work. Joshua's farewell address to the Israelites charged them to renew their covenant with the Lord and continue to seek instruction from his Word (Joshua 23). Paul's last recorded instruction to Timothy includes the exhortation to expound the Word (2 Timothy 4:2). Nehemiah was so zealous for the Word that when he returned to Jerusalem a second time and discovered areas where the people had succumbed to violating the Law that he even pulled out the hair of some of the men (Nehemiah 13:25)!

These same principles can be applied to our lives. First, the clearer we are about the call God has given us, the stronger we will be in fighting the obstacles that accompany it. Much energy is wasted when we waver back and forth as to whether or not we are *really* doing what God wants when we don't see the results we expected. Our determination to stay the course must rest on the assurance that God has called us, not upon our assessment of the fruit. Some fruit doesn't mature for months, years, or perhaps, even in a lifetime. If we need immediate results, we will not be able to overcome the inevitable obstacles. Certainty robs the enemy of a landing strip from which to launch doubts.

The mindset of an overcomer also recognizes that a lifetime of human striving achieves nothing compared to what a soul surrendered to God can accomplish in one day. When difficulty comes, our normal tendencies lean toward taking the situation in our own hands. We either try harder, looking toward natural means to accomplish supernatural goals, or we passively give up altogether. On the other hand, when success does arrive, the temptation to credit ourselves and forget *who* gave us the victory threatens to undo what we've won. The mark of a true conqueror is the mark of humble reliance on God in either trouble or triumph.

Finally, if we do not know the Word of God and revere what it says, it will be impossible to sustain victory. The Word is the *sword* of the spirit (Ephesians 6:17); it cuts through the enemy's assault. If we take it lightly, doubt it, or misuse it, we might as well be wielding a butter knife.

The Mark of Victory

Our church met in a Lion's Club Community Building on Sunday mornings for more years than I care to remember. Although we were grateful for the provision, those of you who have had to rent space on a weekly basis can understand the ongoing frustration of having to set up and tear down chairs, music equipment, and Sunday school rooms. Fringe benefits included sweltering heat in the summer, due to lack of air conditioning, and sticky floors when another group partied in the "sanctuary" the previous night. Limited by the lack of accessibility for midweek gatherings, offices, and any sense of "permanence," we jumped at the chance when a building became available. But there was one catch. The building we wanted to buy was a warehouse in an agricultural zone (meaning that all construction was limited to agriculture-related business).

Although the previous owners had obtained a non-conforming substitution—which permitted them to run a business that was not limited to agriculture—when our church applied for our occupational permit, we were met with fierce resistance. The zoning officer bluntly stated, "That's an agricultural zone. You can't do it." Even when Chip, (our pastor), tried to explain our situation, the response was anything but sympathetic. The officer basically said that if we wanted to waste $200.00 on the application fee it was fine with him. His opposition was so strong that we began to question whether this move really was God's will. We had started with clarity, but his adamancy weakened our resolve. As we continued to pray, however, we sensed we were to push ahead, so we presented our petition before the three-man zoning board. Little did they know that our petition was saturated with reliance on God, not them, for the outcome.

It seemed like half of our church squeezed into the small room where the zoning meeting was held. Even neighbors, who approved of what we were trying to do, came to support us. But the hostility from the board was palpable. One man pointedly said, "We don't want a church there at all." As Chip patiently answered each of their questions, it became increasingly obvious that they had no legal ground to stand upon to keep us from obtaining the building.

The next morning my devotions were from the fourth chapter of Zechariah. "Not by might nor by power, but by my Spirit, says the Lord Almighty. What are you, O mighty mountain? Before Zerubbabel you will become level ground. Then he will bring out the capstone to shouts of 'God bless it! God bless it!'" (4:6–7). It was not a mere coincidence that I read that passage that day. God's Word infused me with faith and eliminated any lingering doubts as to whether or not our plans would succeed.

The zoning board had been a big mountain of intimidation, but the Spirit of the Lord had leveled it. On the night our building was dedicated, shouts of "God bless it!" rang through the countryside.

God's plan for us includes overcoming every obstacle that keeps us from knowing his love so we can bear the mark of victory. He calls us to vanquish, defeat, beat, lick, subdue, reduce, overcome, overthrow, and rout the enemy and all his strongholds. By staying connected to his love, we will fulfill his plan for us to live as *more than conquerors*. And we will leave behind tracks of victory for others to follow.

Perhaps one of the most difficult areas to sustain the mark of victory lies in the challenge to forgive. Yet, as William Blake penned, "The glory of Christianity is to conquer through forgiveness." The next chapter will help us see how.

DIGGING DEEPER

1. What are some of the "things" that threaten to separate you from the love of God?
2. How have you met betrayal and rejection in your life? How has God used betrayal and rejection redemptively?
3. How has a failure prepared you for a bigger plan?
4. Can you think of any "small stuff" in your life that has contributed to feelings of separation from God?
5. How do you respond to the thought expressed in Song of Solomon 4:9—"you have ravished my heart"—as you consider God's love for you?
6. Describe a situation in your life in which the obstacles you faced became the means to victory.
7. Have you experienced a time when you felt your "burnt stones can't live again"? Explain.
8. When has reliance upon God rather than yourself caused you to become more than a conqueror?

CHAPTER 7

A THREE-LEGGED STOOL
THE MARK OF FORGIVENESS

*Willingness to suffer unjustly is the commitment to love uphill, against
all the natural forces that would encourage us not to.*
—Dick Keyes
True Heroism

A NUMBER OF years ago I took a graduate course in psychology at
a local university. It turned out to be an encounter group, the format
being that we sat around in a circle, and each week the professor would
have one or two students "tell their story." On this particular night, one
of the students was talking about his relationship with his father. His
tone revealed apparent bitterness, and at one point, I made the comment
(naïve as I was) that if he wanted to come full circle, he would forgive his
dad. The professor did a double take. With a dismissive air, he looked
at me and said, "That's so *g—d—Christian.*"

To which I replied, "Well, I am one."

"A lot of people say they're Christians," he retorted.

"But I'm a real one."

My candor piqued his curiosity, and he asked if I would be the next
to tell my "story."

I relate this incident to say that I wasn't necessarily thinking of
forgiveness as a *Christian* term. I was just recognizing it as the route to

freedom. But my agnostic professor knew it was a Christian concept. Indeed, Christianity's very foundation is marked with forgiveness.

The definition of forgiveness could be worded as *the voluntary, loving cancellation of a debt.* Initially more of a choice than a feeling, forgiveness declares, "I will no longer hold this against you." When people hurt us, they fall into our debt in a very real sense. We have the option of holding that debt against them, saying "you'll pay," or holding that debt in the light of God's redemptive love and believing that he is able to take the hurt and use it for good in our lives.

Forgiveness is not minimizing the offense or forgetting it happened. It's not trying to make ourselves think that someone who's not nice really isn't that bad. It sees the sin against us for what it is. But it recognizes that on the cross, Jesus paid the debt. He paid the debt we owe to those we have hurt, and he paid the debts owed to us. So we have no reason to continue to exact payment. We've been compensated. Refusing to forgive denies his compensation. That's why forgiveness is ultimately more of an issue between us and God than it is between us and others. The mark of forgiveness indicates the authenticity of our spiritual life.

When I picture forgiveness, I visualize a three-legged stool. A three-legged stool is one that doesn't wobble easily. A chair is stable only when all four legs rest on an even surface. But a three-legged stool remains steady, no matter what kind of ground it rests upon. Cameras sit on tripods to assure stability. In the past, people used three-legged stools when milking cows. And so forgiveness keeps us from wobbling as well. Like that stool, forgiveness is comprised of three essential components. Picture with me a seat on which is written "forgiveness," supported by three legs, each one representing an aspect of forgiveness: *faith, mercy,* and *action.*

Faith

The first leg on the stool is faith. When Jesus was teaching his disciples about forgiveness, he instructed them that even if someone sinned against them seven times in one day— but each time came back and repented—they were to forgive. How did the disciples respond to this instruction? "Increase our faith!" (Luke 17:5). It takes faith to forgive. Psalm 119:50 says, "My comfort in my suffering is this: Your promise preserves my life." When we suffer hurt, rejection, or abuse, we can either be comforted with thoughts of revenge or by the promises of God. The first brings death, the second, life.

The story of Joseph in Genesis 37–50 so well illustrates the second choice. Although he was the favorite of his father, Joseph was not the favorite of his brothers. Their jealousy consumed them to such an extent that when the opportunity presented itself, they sold him to slave traders headed for Egypt. Joseph was separated from family and enslaved in a foreign land, yet he refused to hold a grudge against his brothers. Nowhere in Scripture does it record that he nursed feelings of anger or bitterness. He somehow managed to "make the best" of his forced enslavement. How did he do that? He held on to the promises God had given him through dreams.

Joseph had once dreamed he was in the field with his brothers binding sheaves of grain. Suddenly, his grain stood upright while all their sheaves bowed down to his. Then he had another dream, where the sun, moon, and eleven stars all bowed down to him. The implication of the dreams was clear, and despite the increased jealousy it provoked in his brothers, and even the rebuke from his father, Joseph believed the dreams (Genesis 37:5–10). When the *exact opposite* occurred, and he was sold into slavery, he looked beyond his circumstances and held on, in faith, to what would assuredly come to pass. That's why he could declare years later, when in fact his brothers did bow down to him, "You intended to harm me, but God intended it for good to accomplish what is now being done, the saving of many lives" (Genesis 50:20).

Revenge on his brothers would have been a shallow, puny goal. Joseph was bigger than that. This is not to say he didn't have to go through a process to get to that point. His life in Egypt was anything but smooth sailing. He had suffered through false accusations, imprisonment, and broken promises. But even before the ultimate fulfillment of the dream, Joseph's faith permeated his outlook. After the birth of his second son, Ephraim (which in Hebrew sounds like *twice blessed*), he declared, "God has made me fruitful in the land of my suffering" (Genesis 41:52). He recognized that God's hand had been upon him. God had used it all to make Joseph the great man he came to be—great not only in position, but also in heart when he forgave his brothers. Holding on to the promise not only had preserved his life, but also had enabled him to accomplish all that God had planned.

Faith and forgiveness are intricately woven together. They always propel us on, to what is ahead. Joseph looked forward, and that enabled him to deal with the injustice of the present. Unforgiveness always looks behind; it keeps us tied to the past. We blame our current condition on what has happened in earlier days or years. Such an outlook is fostered by a *slave mentality.*

A slave mentality is what Israel maintained after leaving Egypt. Even though they had been delivered from their bondage, the nation continued to identify themselves with slavery: *I'm oppressed; therefore, I am.* Their minds had not been renewed. For example, they had no concept of an authority figure valuing and caring for them. All they had experienced from authority in Egypt was exploitation. The taskmasters had one purpose—to make their lives miserable while getting as much work out of them as possible. So when something went wrong in the desert, they *looked back* to what they had known and transferred their distorted concept of authority to their conception of God.

Even though they had been spared from all the plagues—gnats, frogs, locusts, flies, boils, darkness, death of their firstborn—they quickly dismissed God's miracle-working power. Within days of escaping Egypt, when they reached the barrier of the Red Sea, they *looked back* to their slavery rather than forward to the promise. "Better to serve the Egyptians than die in the desert," they complained (Exodus 14:12). Later, when the food started to run out, the whole community grumbled. They *looked back* and saw only "pots of meat" and "all the food they wanted" (Exodus 16:3). Then when the water supply was drained, they again *looked back* to the days of their slavery for comfort (Exodus 17:3).

Things were tough for the Israelites, there's no doubt about that. They encountered difficult, stressful days in the desert. But rather than remembering past faithfulness and believing in the promises, they reverted back to being a suspicious, slave-mentality driven people. The slave mentality colored their recollection of what life in Egypt had been like. The reality was that they were treated brutally. They had cried out to God again and again to deliver them and take them back to their land. Now, they were angry and suspect, practically demanding to go back to everything that had enslaved them.

When we experience hurtful or demeaning situations, we sometimes react more like slaves than sons. Forgetting the promise that because we are children of God there is nothing anyone *really* can do to harm us, we embrace a slave mentality that chains us to our past wounds. When we fail to forgive, we actually assign more power to the one who hurt us than we do to God. Yet God is the one who has the power to work all things together for our good (Romans 8:28)—even injustices, abuses, insults, and injuries. How can we withhold forgiveness from someone who has harmed us when God has *promised* to override the effect? "If God is for us, who can be against us?" Paul declares in Romans 8:31. Faith in that redemptive truth is the first leg of the stool.

Mercy

Without mercy, there can be no forgiveness. It's the leg of the stool that both helps us to see ourselves and that most visibly marks us with forgiveness. If we don't realize how much we have received forgiveness and mercy, it will be much harder to release mercy and forgiveness to others. The Lord's Prayer teaches us to ask God for forgiveness of our debts on the basis that we have forgiven those indebted to us. Jesus goes on to say clearly that if we don't forgive, we won't be forgiven (Matthew 6:15).

In a scene from *The Merchant of Venice*, Shakespeare describes the virtue of mercy in a compelling way. The lawyer, Portia, is pleading for mercy on behalf of the defendant. But the accuser is out for revenge. He had loaned him money with the stipulation that if it was not repaid in a specific amount of time, the borrower would be put to death. Even when someone else offered to pay the debt, the accuser would have none of it. So Portia makes this eloquent plea:

> The quality of mercy is not strained;
> It droppeth as the gentle rain from heaven
> Upon the place beneath. It is twice blest:
> It blesseth him that gives and him that takes.
> 'Tis mightiest in the mightiest; it becomes

The throned monarch better than his crown;
His scepter shows the force of temporal power,
The attribute to awe and majesty,
Wherein doth sit the dread and fear of kings;
But mercy is above this sceptred sway,
It is enthroned in the hearts of kings,
It is an attribute of God himself;
And earthly power doth then show likest God's
When mercy seasons justice....[27]

A tremendous power is unleashed through mercy... a "twice blest" virtue, blessing the one who gives it as well as the one who receives. When we demand justice from someone who has hurt us, insisting we get our "pound of flesh," we forget our own cries for mercy—without which, we wouldn't be saved.

Matthew 18 relates the familiar parable of the unmerciful servant. When this servant refused to forgive the debt owed to him after he had just been forgiven of his debt, the punishment was severe. "'Shouldn't you have had mercy on your fellow servant just as I had on you?' In anger his master turned him over to the jailers to be tortured, until he should pay back all he owed" (verses 33–34). When we refuse to forgive, we actually create a prison within, and the jailers of guilt, fear, bitterness, and anger torture us. Satan, the great "accuser of the brethren," will attempt to keep us in the prison of our accusations. He'll whisper demands for justice and remind us of the insults we've received, resulting in more and more bondage. But mercy is the "get-out-of-jail-free" card.

Carl Carter is a man who received it. (Note: the following story is true, but the names have been changed.) Carl and Dixie were friends of my parents throughout my school years. Their kids went to my school, where Dixie worked as a secretary. Carl was a hard type of man. He didn't encourage his wife much, and he was extremely critical of everything she and the kids did. Starved for affection and affirmation, Dixie ended up having an affair with the school principal. To make matters worse, this principal was a preacher and Sunday school teacher. He was also married with children.

News of an incident like that traveled fast in a small town like ours, and it wasn't long before Carl learned of the affair. He and Dixie divorced, their family pretty much destroyed. Eventually the affair ended, but Carl was never the same. I hadn't seen him in well over twenty years, but when I returned home after my grandmother died, he came to her viewing. I never would have recognized him. He had always been a thin man; now he was probably close to 300 pounds. He was plagued with a number of serious physical ailments: prostate problems, knots in his legs, and complications with his lungs that were so severe that he had to use a breathing machine. Unforgiveness had taken its toll.

Since my dad's salvation, he and Carl had spent a lot of time talking about God. But Carl said that every time he thought about accepting the Lord, the preacher's face would come up in his mind and he couldn't let go of the anger and bitterness.

Dixie, however, had made her life right with Christ. And she felt convicted to write Carl a letter. It was the first letter she had written to him in twenty-eight years. In the letter she admitted how wrong she had been and how sorry she was for what she had done to the family. She expressed concern for his soul, and she encouraged him to listen to what my dad had to say.

That letter broke Carl. He called my dad and cried, "I want to get saved, but I don't know what to do. Will you help me?" Dad rushed to his house and led him in a prayer of repentance; Carl confessed his wrongs and expressed forgiveness toward all those—including the preacher—who had hurt him. Dixie's act of mercy had opened the door for Carl's salvation. At seventy-five years old, Carl had finally found peace. Such is the power of forgiveness when mercy triumphs over judgment.

How do we view God's mercy? Do we really see God's forgiveness in all the stupid things we do? Or do we think he's judging us for not measuring up to some invisible standard of perfection? We will never be able to forgive unless we recognize God's relentless mercy toward us. If we perceive God to be constantly dissatisfied because of our mistakes and inadequacies, we will feel guilty, and in effect, pass those feelings of judgment on to others who "break the rules." But if we experience the release of knowing God's mercy, it actually empowers us to change. In the end we don't fall as much as we did before. And when we extend mercy to others who don't deserve it any more than we do, they, too, are empowered to change. They and we find release from the prison of judgment.

Action

The third leg of the stool is action. Sometimes it's only in the *action* of forgiveness that we realize whether or not we have actually forgiven someone. James 1:22 reads, "Do not merely listen to the word, and so deceive yourselves. *Do* what it says" (emphasis mine). If we are unable to demonstrate some form of kindness to someone who has hurt us, we should question the sincerity of our forgiveness. Action completes forgiveness. Sometimes that action involves doing the exact opposite of what we feel.

I was once talking with a woman who was frustrated because her husband was doing a poor job of leading the family. Her tendency was to throw up her hands in disgust and let the walls build between them. But instead, she started doing the opposite of what she felt. She intentionally started serving him and being kind, even though he didn't *deserve* it. As it turned out, not only did it set her free, but it actually made it easier for him to change. Performing acts of kindness towards those who have hurt us stimulates the reality of forgiveness in our lives.

Some may object that it is hypocritical to act on something we don't feel. And it could be at times. But if we are acting in obedience to what the Lord has commanded us to do, it is not hypocrisy. It has to do with the motives of our hearts. Those Jesus referred to as hypocrites were the Pharisees, who performed the right outward actions, but for the purpose of looking superior to others. That's a very different thing than what we're talking about here. Nowhere does God give us commands in the Scripture that are prefaced with a concern as to how we feel about doing them. *When you feel like it, you shall have no other gods before me. When you feel like it, you shall not commit adultery. When you feel like it, you shall not covet.* I don't think so. In fact, the way to resist temptation often lies in *not* doing what we feel like doing.

It reminds me of the oft-told story of an experience that Corrie ten Boom had years after she was released from the Nazi concentration camp. She was speaking in a church when she spotted one of the S.S. guards who had been responsible for so many brutal deaths. He approached her after the service to thank her for her message and to relay how grateful he was that Jesus had taken away his sins. He extended his hand to her, but at that moment, Corrie froze. All the pain of that terrible time came rushing back, and she literally could not lift her hand to meet his. Realizing she could not forgive him in and of herself, she asked Jesus to give her his forgiveness for the man. Finally, she *took his hand*, and with that *action* came an overwhelming flood of love for this former Nazi.[28]

Sometimes the *action* of forgiveness isn't just forgiving the offenses of others. It also can involve taking responsibility for our part of the disagreement. Even if we have only contributed to one fourth of the problem and the other person is three quarters in the wrong, God may ask us to be the one to initiate the forgiveness process. Chip and I had only been married two weeks when the Lord began revealing this principle to me. We were living in Boulder, Colorado, and on Friday nights we would often go to youth services at a large church in Denver. We didn't really know anyone there, but we enjoyed the music and the teaching. On this particular evening, a stranger came up to me after the service and said, "Sister, I believe I'm to give you this book." It was a book I was unfamiliar with at the time, *The Calvary Road* by Roy Hession. I was a little taken aback, but I politely received the book, not really knowing whether or not I would read it.

On the way home from the service, Chip and I got into a huge hassle. The particulars of the argument have long been forgotten, but I remember the feeling of devastation. As soon as we reached our apartment, I was out the door. I wanted to walk—anywhere— just to be alone. I cried and I prayed, wondering how God could have led me into such a disastrous relationship. I was drenched in self-pity. My only comfort came in the thought of how worried Chip must be. By now, he was probably even considering calling the police to help him find me! So I returned home, convinced I would be gracious as he begged for my forgiveness. But, he didn't *beg* for my forgiveness. He didn't ask. He didn't say anything at all. He was fast asleep! That put enough oil on the fire to keep the anger burning throughout the next day. We barely spoke, except for the polite "excuse me" kind of remarks that you use when you want to let someone know there's a distance.

By evening, Chip was back in our bedroom and I was sitting in the living room. Then I happened to glance at *The Calvary Road*. I picked it up and began reading about the necessity of dying to ourselves if we are to live Christ-centered lives.[29] Page after page seemed to reveal a new aspect of brokenness, and page after page convicted me of my wrong attitude. Finally, I went back to the bedroom and simply said, "Chip, I'm sorry." That's all it took. The mountain that had built between us crumbled as he confessed his wrong as well.

Clearly, for forgiveness to take place, I had to *do* something. I had to humble myself, walk back to the bedroom, and tell Chip I was wrong. Without that *action*, forgiveness could not have occurred. It was an action, by the way, that would be repeated many times in the next years, a necessary action in order to keep walking on *The Calvary Road*.

Final Thoughts

Let me conclude this chapter by reiterating a few specific points about forgiveness.

First, it's important that we see our need to forgive; as Christians it's not optional. We are commanded to forgive because not forgiving interferes with our relationship with God. There have been times in my life where it wasn't love for the person but for God that motivated me to forgive. I couldn't stand the separation from him that my unforgiveness brought.

Second, ask for God's help if you are struggling to forgive. C. S. Lewis said, "Everyone thinks forgiveness is a lovely idea until they have something to forgive."[30] Forgiveness is more difficult than we think, but it is not impossible. Everyone has different levels or thresholds of forgiveness, similar to thresholds of pain. Some people can tolerate more pain than others; some people let offenses roll off easier. But whatever our thresholds, we all come to places where we have to ask God to help us. We need *his* forgiveness to flow through us because ours is inadequate.

Third, don't withdraw when someone has hurt you. I know this is the natural response for many of us. But try running to the roar. Do the opposite of what you *feel*. Be willing to follow any little nudge of kindness you might be directed to do. Or you be the one to take responsibility to say you're sorry for whatever part you may have played in the disagreement. It doesn't happen naturally. It's easy for the threat of even more hurt to dissuade us. Pastor Tim Keller points out that "forgiveness always comes at a cost to the one granting the forgiveness."[31] Yet paying the price thrusts us into the very heart of Christ.

There is only one who doesn't want you to forgive, and that one is the enemy of your soul. Don't align yourself with him. Nothing can mar the tracks you leave behind more than unforgiveness. If you want to leave a clearly-marked path that is worthy of emulation, don't let strains of bitterness distort your tracks. If you let your steps be saturated in the faith, mercy, and action that forgiveness requires, the impression you leave will direct many to the path of life.

Perhaps extending forgiveness requires us to drink more deeply from the well of God's grace than any other act of obedience. Yet grace provides the power we need to walk through the process. And so we turn toward yet another mark to help us mirror his character, the mark of grace.

DIGGING DEEPER

1. How is forgiveness like *loving uphill*?
2. How would you define forgiveness? Do you recognize any faulty concepts in your understanding of forgiveness?
3. Why do you think it takes faith to forgive?
4. How does mercy release us and others from the prison of judgment?
5. Can you give an example of a time in your life when you saw an action complete forgiveness?
6. How can "feelings" hinder the work of forgiveness?
7. Have there been times when you have had to ask God to *help* you forgive? What has been the result?
8. Are there any "special needs" people in your life waiting for your forgiveness?

CHAPTER 8

BETTER THAN I DESERVE
THE MARK OF GRACE

*Until we embrace this costly grace—or rather until we allow ourselves
to be embraced by it—we can never know what it means to be
completely accepted.*

—Michael Card
A Violent Grace

A WHILE BACK I received a letter from a girl who used to live with
us. Now married with three young children, she serves as a missionary in
China. Her note broke my heart. In it, she explained her take on grace.
She wrote, "*I still don't get it.* And I'm married to someone who thinks
grace is something that took place at the cross—cancelled the debt—but
it isn't an ongoing, daily experience. So we both tend to be driven,
goal-oriented, always examining ourselves, and never satisfied. I know in
my head that God cares more about what goes on in my heart through
the course of a day than he cares about what I get done…but I always
feel like I'm falling short. It's very difficult for me to not think of each
day as a success/failure…I'm beating a punching bag, wearing myself
out; and my enemy is standing behind me chuckling." Anyone relate to
my friend's dilemma? Do you ever struggle with *getting grace*?

We all know those people who exhibit that distinguishable mark
of grace. They are free from self-consciousness, generous, kind, and
understanding. They work, but without striving. They've escaped the

vanity of their accomplishments because they have never lost their first love. Oswald Chambers describes them when he writes, "The idea is not that [they] work for God, but that [they] are so loyal to Him that He can do His work through [them]."[32] Those marked with grace have acquired a keen awareness that they have fared *far better than they deserve*, no matter what their circumstances. Their gratitude positions them for noble, lasting works.

Grace stands at the beginning and end of our Christian walk. As John Newton penned, "Tis grace that brought me safe this far, and grace will lead me home." Every one of Paul's epistles opens and closes with grace:

- Romans 1:7 and 16:20
- 1 Corinthians 1:3 and 16:23
- 2 Corinthians 1:2 and 13:14
- Galatians 1:3 and 6:18
- Ephesians 1:2 and 6:24
- Philippians 1:2 and 4:23
- Colossians 1:2 and 4:18
- 1 Thessalonians 1:1 and 5:28
- 2 Thessalonians 1:2 and 3:18
- 1 Timothy 1:2 and 6:21
- 2 Timothy 1:2 and 4:22
- Titus 1:4 and 3:15
- Philemon 3 and 25

Grace expresses the favor, kindness, and tenderness of God. It is the undeserved empowering of God through Jesus Christ. Without grace none of us could have entered the kingdom; without grace, none of us can remain. Yet, vital as it is, our experience of God's grace may diminish as we seek to "work out our salvation with fear and trembling" (Philippians 2:12). Paul urged his fellow workers "not to receive God's grace in vain" (2 Corinthians 6:1). I'm afraid that all too often many of us do just that. Our lifestyles render his grace ineffective. We join ranks with a society propelled by pressure and performance rather than be yoked to the one who teaches us how to walk in the "unforced rhythms of grace" (Matthew 11:28), as Eugene Peterson puts it in *The Message*. So what causes us to receive his grace in vain? How can we ensure that the mark of grace will remain fixed, and in fact, *lead us home*?

We Receive the Grace of God in Vain When We Forget How Much We Need It

The prerequisite for drinking in the grace of God rests in knowing how terribly flawed we really are. Some of us have a tendency to think that the more mature we become, the less we need the grace of God. But although we may *sin less*, we remain far from being *sinless*. In fact, the saints who have gone on before us testify that the closer they drew to God, the more acutely aware they became of their sinful nature. They discovered that when they were tempted to lie down and quit, it was the grace of God, not some internal fortitude, that empowered them to stand, walk, and even run again. They were humble enough to admit that there were times when it was not the strength of their grip on God but his grasp on their outstretched arms that held them. They realized how much they *didn't* deserve God's grace, and it was this awareness that enabled them to receive it. So their dependency on grace grew, not lessened. John Bradford was one such man.

Bradford served as a British royal chaplain in the 1500s. He traveled throughout England, teaching the doctrines of the Reformation. Men came to Christ wherever he went, so great was the power of his witness. The now common phrase, "But for the grace of God, there go I," originated with Bradford. He is said to have repeated those words every time he observed the execution of a convict. He maintained that perspective of grace in a unique way. He listed his worst sins on paper so that they would be in his view during private prayer. It reminded him to offer God a contrite spirit and a thankful heart for his salvation. He would then pray for grace to serve God wholeheartedly. When he was burned at the stake with another young man, his final words rang with the grace that had characterized his life. "Be of good comfort, brother, for we shall have a merry supper with the Lord this night."[33] He died in peace because he had kept his focus not on what he accomplished, but on the grace he'd received in order *to* accomplish.

After we've been Christians for a few years and we begin to experience the transforming power of redemption, we can tend to forget how far we've come. We can think we were always this generous, this loving, this *good*. But we deceive ourselves. Although we are not to wallow in a mire of low self-esteem or false modesty, a failure to remember who we were before Christ, distances us from the mark of grace.

The apostle Paul never forgot where he came from. A self-proclaimed zealot for the law, he had been so enmeshed in pride, legalism, and religion that he had missed the Messiah he was seeking. Paul was one of the most confident men in all of Scripture... "If anyone else thinks he has reasons to put confidence in the flesh, I have more…a Hebrew of Hebrews; in regard to the law, a Pharisee; as for zeal, persecuting the church; as for legalistic righteousness, faultless" (Philippians 3:4–6). Yet he proclaimed it was only "through Christ" that he received the strength to do all things (Philippians 4:13). He considered the *best* of his efforts as *rubbish* compared to the "surpassing greatness of knowing Christ" (Philippians 3:4–8). He was able to suffer much for the gospel because he knew there was no hardship he would suffer that could compensate for what Christ did for him on the cross.

Sometimes God presents us with challenges so great that we have no other alternative than to draw from his grace. My husband was acutely reminded of his need for grace when he traveled to the former Soviet Union on a short-term mission trip a few years ago. Bibles were still being confiscated at the border, and Christians were just beginning to be allowed to meet freely in public places. A great deal of tension remained throughout the country as the underground church cautiously started to emerge.

On one occasion, Chip and his other three team members held an outdoor meeting in a park outside of Riga. After he finished preaching, a woman came up to him, and through an interpreter, asked if he would pray for her because she was deaf. Now God had never used Chip to minister a supernatural healing before, but he knew he could not refuse to bring this poor woman's need before the Lord. So he prayed in the best way he knew how, and God, in his grace, moved. The woman began crying and jumping up and down. She could hear!

The next day, another meeting was held, and 1,000 people showed up for the service. When they realized Chip was the one who had prayed for the woman, all 1,000 seemed to press toward him, asking for prayer. It resulted in one of the most profound experiences in Chip's life. As he prayed for them one by one, shouts of praise erupted throughout the crowd. Healings were taking place as soon as he finished praying. There was no doubt in Chip's mind as to the source of the miracles. God's power was made perfect through a weak but willing vessel.

Seeing how much we continue to need God's grace is not a sign of immaturity. On the contrary, it's an awareness that protects us from the illusion of our own greatness.

We Receive the Grace of God in Vain When We Revert To Self-effort

King Saul stands in Scripture as a prime example of one who was destroyed by self-reliance. In 1 Samuel 15 we read about how Saul offered sacrifices to God after winning a battle against the Amalekites. He had been instructed to sacrifice *everything*; instead, he spared the Amalekite king and all the best sheep and cattle "…everything that was good" (verse 9). Saul sacrificed *as he saw fit*. Samuel's directives to destroy everything obviously didn't make sense to him. But rather than drawing on the grace of God to obey something he didn't understand, he followed his own inclinations.

If we're not careful, we can fall into the same trap. We may be willing to give God our sins, weaknesses, and shortcomings, but when it comes to our *good stuff*, we balk, especially if God is asking us to do something we don't understand. The truth is that the "Saul" in us wants to take credit for *something*. And clearly, that was Saul's motivation.

Saul's life illustrates three fatal consequences of self-effort: pride, comparison with others, and a negation of faith. Immediately after the battle, Saul went to Carmel to "set up a monument in his own honor…" (1 Samuel 15:12). He quickly forgot that it was the grace of God that had given him the victory in the first place. His pride drove him to take the credit. But there's not room for two monuments in the kingdom of God. The Scripture warns us that all our boasting should be in the Lord. Are you smart? Thank God for the intelligence he's given you. Are you a hard worker? Give God glory that you were trained properly. Are you wealthy? Be grateful for the abilities and the opportunities you've received. Grace enables us to see that we would be nothing and have nothing at all if it weren't for God. Self-effort, on the other hand, lusts for the glory that says, "Look what I did."

Self-effort breeds insecurity, and insecurity thrusts us into a constant comparison with others in an attempt to evaluate how we measure up. Rather than focusing on the assignment given to him, Saul constantly compared himself to David, resulting in a jealousy that drove him to madness. Comparing ourselves to others may not make us insane, but it is definitely a lose/lose situation. It inevitably causes us to fall either to pride (our work's better than theirs) or inferiority (their work's better than ours), which are both reflections of self-effort. In the end, it is the faithfulness to our task that will count more than man's relative estimation of success.

We have some friends who have been missionaries in France most of their lives. Their work has been long and tedious, and they have seen only a handful of converts in the years they have served. Yet, by grace, they have remained faithful to their call. We've known others in ministry who would be considered highly successful, yet who's to say which ones are walking in greater obedience? In our culture, *bigger* has become equated with *better,* and as a result, many in smaller works have had to fight discouragement and doubt. But it shouldn't be this way. It is a waste of time and energy to compare ourselves to others. Even the disciples had to be reminded of this. When Peter asked Jesus about John, Jesus didn't mince words. He told him that John was not his concern. Peter's job was to *follow him* (John 21:22). And so is ours.

Finally, self-effort leads to a negation of faith. It is impossible to believe God to bring something about if we are striving to do it ourselves. Saul again serves as an example. In an earlier conflict with the Philistines, recorded in 1 Samuel 13, Saul had been told to wait for Samuel to offer sacrifices to the Lord *before* engaging in battle. But when his anxious troops were overcome with fear, Saul disregarded the command of the Lord. He didn't have the faith to believe Samuel would come in time, so he offered the sacrifices himself. When Samuel did finally arrive, he rebuked Saul and told him that his foolish actions would cost him the kingdom (verse 14). Saul had refused the grace that would have helped him to believe and obey. But that's what self-effort always does. Andrew Murray explains why we so often fail to move from self-reliance to faith: "...there is a secret root of evil which must be removed. That root is the spirit of bondage, the legal spirit of self-effort, which hinders that humble faith that knows that God will work all, and yields to Him to do it."[34] Grace releases us from that bondage and enables us to wait upon the promises of God.

I saw an example of how self-effort was defeated on Tangier Island, Virginia, in 1995. On our twenty-fifth wedding anniversary, Chip and I hopped on a mail boat and visited Tangier, a remote island on the Chesapeake. Unknown to us at the time, three years earlier, Tangier Island had been the recipient of an outpouring of God's grace. No, Billy Graham hadn't conducted an evangelistic crusade and neither had Luis Palau. The two churches on the island simply joined together for what was to be a one-week series of meetings. Six weeks later, two thirds of the island's 600 residents had come to know Christ as Lord.

Among the new converts was Betty Bee. Betty Bee was the epitome of self-reliance. Owner of the Chesapeake House, Betty was a hard-headed business woman, successful, not thinking she needed anyone or anything. But one morning as she met with her employees, she found them unusually animated. She asked them what was going on, and they reported that all but two of them had been saved in the last week. The revival had erupted, and Betty wanted to find out what all the fuss was about. So she went to church that night.

Betty determined that she would walk right out the door of the church if someone dared to ask her to go to the altar. No one was going to manipulate her into anything. But by the time the service was over, her pounding heart was so loud that she was sure everyone around her could hear it. She vowed to her nephew, who had accompanied her, that she would never go back and experience that again. He retorted that God wouldn't want them anyway. *God wouldn't want her?* Something about his words stung her. She has no recollection of what she did the rest of the night. She only remembers that she wrestled until the morning hours.

The next day, every Christian in her family came to visit her, even though they had no idea of the tumult going on within. It was too much for Betty's resistance. By evening, she couldn't wait to go to church. As the preacher opened the meeting, he said, "You don't have to wait until after the preaching to come to the altar." It was a good thing, because that was all the encouragement Betty Bee needed. She literally ran to the altar and fell to her knees, accepting Christ as Lord. What followed was a total transformation of her life. One whisper of God's grace quieted all the turbulence that had been produced by a life of self-effort and reliance. Betty Bee was born again.

We Receive the Grace of God in Vain When We Fail To See that It Works

To me, one of the most intriguing passages of Scripture is found in Titus 2:11–12. It says, "For the grace of God that brings salvation has appeared to all men. It teaches us to say 'No' to ungodliness and worldly passions, and to live self-controlled, upright and godly lives...." This scripture tells us that the empowerment we need to live righteously cannot be found in a set of legalistic do's and don'ts but in the experience of God's grace. Without grace, our lives are more *uptight* than *upright*, and everyone around us suffers because of it. Donald Miller writes that the problem with the Christian culture is that we think of love as a commodity. We use love like money, "withholding affirmation from those who disagree with us, but lavishly financing the ones who don't."[35] If we really want to see someone change, rather than standing back in judgment, maybe at times we should be pouring out grace and love extravagantly.

Some of the most potent experiences I've had involved "grace moments" of either receiving or giving grace. My husband says "yes" to something he'd rather say "no" to, not because I manipulated him, but because he wants to please me; and it makes me want to please him all the more. My daughter is in a *bad mood*, but rather than jumping in with condemnation, I find ways to serve her, and her attitude shifts. My son lands in a place where the "rule book" could be thrown at him, but the school principal instead affirms his integrity, and my son responds with a new level of maturity.

Honestly, I haven't fully grasped how grace works. I think of how I used to feel that my personal mission in life was to right every wrong and address every injustice. It didn't leave a lot of room for grace. And it was not the way God had dealt with me. He let me go close to the edge when I was trying to find out what was real and what wasn't. He didn't say, "You better not live in Colorado and hang out with hippies and read Eastern philosophy or you might forget the cross." He knew just how far to let me go so I could discover who I was, who he was, and how it all fit together. His tremendous grace didn't try to control me or manipulate me or squeeze me into a one-size-fits-all box! When I realized how well he knew me and how much he loved me, it made me want to give back to him my wholehearted devotion. I don't know how, but his grace worked. Thankfully, its working was not and is not dependent on my understanding.

We Receive the Grace of God in Vain When We Fail To See the Connection between Grace and Works

Many wrestle with a grace/works dilemma. If we are saved freely by grace, and grace is meant to be our ongoing *modus operandi*, where do works fit in? Works comprise a major part of our Christian walk. James 2:17 tells us that "faith without works is dead." And Ephesians 2:10 says that "we are God's workmanship, created in Christ Jesus to do good works, which God prepared in advance for us to do." How do we put forth the effort to perform those good works and avoid slipping out of grace? In our confusion, grace and works get framed as a choice: either we rest in grace or strain in works. It seems today that many Christians are either like my friends in China who exhaust themselves from striving, or like those who find so much security in grace that they do nothing. Those who do nothing subscribe to what Dietrich Bonhoeffer refers to as *cheap grace*, "grace without discipleship, grace without the Cross."[36]

In reality, grace and works do not present an either/or predicament. They flow together, bringing an extraordinary means of resolution when works *express* grace. When our works are not a response to grace, we easily fall into a works frame of mind that puts us on a treadmill of always having to work harder to gain approval from God or man. But it can never satisfy our need for acceptance, because works were never intended to serve that purpose. Sooner or later, those who live in this framework will burn out. Without a concept of grace, the works come across as legalistic and hollow, and that's because they are!

Grace frees us to see that we don't have to do anything to earn God's approval because Christ earned it for us on the cross. When we dilute his sacrifice by mixing it with our works, we make a mockery of the high price he paid to secure our freedom. We negate the truth that *his* work accomplished what *our* work could never do in positioning us to receive God's favor. Paul forcefully reminded the Galatians that if righteousness could be gained through the law, then Christ's death amounted to nothing! (Galatians 2:21).

We will never *get grace* unless we *get the cross.* In his book, *Violent Grace,* Michael Card movingly describes how it took a violent sacrifice to deliver us from ourselves.[37] It took the agony of the cross to stir up the revolution necessary for our hearts to change. It took the brutality of the crucifixion to both convict us and comfort us as we gaze upon the price paid for our sin. If we were to join hymn writer Isaac Watts and "survey the wondrous cross," let ourselves see "sorrow and love flow mingled down," and view the thorns that "compose so rich a crown," then perhaps we, too, would count our "richest gain…but loss and pour contempt on all [our] pride." Grace is the refrain that resounds from the power of the cross. Works embody our grateful response.

We Receive the Grace of God in Vain When We Don't Offer It to Others

The inherent nature of grace calls us to give what we've received. "And God is able to make *all* grace abound to you so that in *all* things at *all* times, having *all* that you need, you will abound in every good work" (2 Corinthians 9:8, emphasis mine). All, all, all, all—the picture is one of overflow. God grants us a rich provision of grace so that the good works he calls us to do will be amply supplied. Abundant grace results in abundant works; little grace yields few works. This passage charges us to let grace saturate every facet of our lives so that we can extend it in every area we touch.

No one has influenced my spiritual life more than Grandpa Creech. Grandpa exuded grace as few people I've ever known. He pastored a small church in southern Ohio for over sixty years, and he spent his life preaching, visiting the sick, conducting funerals and weddings, and taking the gospel to homes throughout the county in his full-time work as a lineman for the telephone company. He never missed an opportunity to display God's grace. I remember one time when a couple came to his door asking if he would marry them. The woman actually smoked a cigarette while he performed the ceremony in his living room!

As he and Grandma grew older, Alzheimer's disease began its slow encroachment on Grandma's life. When it was no longer feasible for her to live at home, plans were made to move her to a nursing facility. But Grandpa's love ran so deep for his bride that he refused to let her go alone. So at ninety-one years old he left both his independence and the house he had built for them on Maple Street in order to be by her side. It seemed, however, that from that time on his own health deteriorated rapidly. In his last year, he could no longer walk, was unable to read his Bible, and could barely speak. Yet the same kind, generous spirit would still shine through to all those who visited him. Some people, when they get older, tend to get hardened, as if calcified in weaknesses that were never resolved in earlier years. Not Grandpa. As his hardships increased, he actually became softer. I believe it was because he had allowed grace to permeate his life.

Even in death the grace that had prevailed throughout his life expressed itself in one final work. In the last months before Grandpa died, he had been unable to speak at all. That's what made the end so powerful. The nurse who was with him told us what happened before he took his last breath. The restlessness and labored breathing suddenly stopped, and a great look of peace came over his face. He lifted his head up from his pillow, and as his eyes focused on some great, unseen reality, Grandpa uttered clearly, "Lord God in heaven!" The nurse, a back-slidden Christian, was shaken. She confessed that Grandpa's witness caused her to realize it was time for her to rethink her life.

Grace had continued to do its work through this great servant of God, and when it was time, it *had led Grandpa home.* And so it will for us, if we embrace this crucial mark and not take it in vain.

Grandpa epitomized the mark of grace to me. He was a flesh-and-blood example of God's gracious nature. Others on my journey have likewise increased my understanding of the many aspects of God's character. Take mothers. From day one, they are about compassion. We learn more about the nature of God's compassion through mothers than most of us realize. So let's look at the mark of compassion and—*what we learn from moms.*

DIGGING DEEPER

1. Have you ever struggled with "getting grace?" How?
2. What has helped you to remember how much you need the grace of God?
3. Describe a situation where you have been challenged to rely on God rather than on your own efforts.
4. Give an example of how the grace of God has taught you to say "no" to ungodliness.
5. Have you ever wrestled with a grace/works dilemma? How have you resolved it?
6. Do you agree with the concept that grace is "violent"? Why or why not?
7. How has the experience of grace in your life prompted you to give to others?
8. Which of the five reasons discussed as to how we receive the grace of God in vain most describes you? How do you plan to change it?

CHAPTER 9

WHAT WE LEARN FROM MOMS
THE MARK OF COMPASSION

Everything I am or ever hope to be, I owe to my angel Mother.
—Abraham Lincoln

MY PARENTS DIVORCED when I was eleven years old, leaving my mother with the formidable task of raising her two children alone. She worked hard as a sales clerk, but even with the help my grandparents provided, money was always tight. Mom never wanted us to think of ourselves as "poor," so she did everything she could to ensure a sense of middle-class normalcy. Although I didn't realize it at the time, she would often sacrifice money she had set aside for her week's lunches so that I could go to the Shake Shoppe and get ice cream with my friends. Throughout my high school years— when being a cheerleader and River Days queen took precedent over all else—she loved me in spite of my vanity. When I went through my "hippie" days in Boulder and started trying out new ideas, she graciously accepted my "enlightened" gift to her of a year's subscription to *Ms. Magazine.* And when Chip and I said we were going to Switzerland to study and didn't know when we'd be back, she was able to let me go.

God, in his sovereignty, uses mothers, fathers, children, rivers, rocks, lambs, and light to reflect different aspects of his nature. But compassion is one facet that is particularly demonstrated through mothers. As they mirror this vital attribute, it reminds all believers that if we desire to reveal Christ, we, too, need to bear the mark of compassion.

I have two children, Bethany and Josiah, and they would be the first to tell you what a sappy mom I am. We're talking sentimental even to the point of foolishness (on occasion). Bethany used to sing "Butterfly Kisses" to me just to watch me cry! I'll never forget the day she received her acceptance for college. I had just gotten out of the shower, complete with a bathrobe and a towel wrapped around my head. We were all thrilled. I was literally jumping up and down with excitement. Then, I guess the reality that she would be leaving home hit me, and I suddenly burst into tears. Through my uncontrollable sobs, I somehow still managed to choke out, "I'm so happy for you," and I meant it. But what a spectacle of inconsistency I must have been, all because of the *sap factor*.

Then there was the time at the end of the school year that Josiah made the comment of how happy he was that summer was here because it left more time for him to love me. Chip and Bethany were practically gagging when he said it, but not me. I fell for it hook, line, and sinker—just like I always fell for his "interrupting walking stick" joke (a variation of the "interrupting cow"). It got to the point where people laughed more at me laughing at his joke than at the joke itself! Well, I'm sure God is not as sappy as me, but I believe he has chosen to reveal at least some aspects of his compassion through mothers, because he knew that at times we would need flesh and blood reminders to show us how it's done.

Both men and women are created in the likeness of God, purposed to reflect his image. But we display that image in different ways. I was talking to my friend Theresa a while back. She was concerned about her then ten-year-old son. She had dropped Andrew off at Boy Scout camp; however, he didn't want to stay. Sympathetic to his tears, she would have agreed to let him skip camp and come home. But not the dad. Tom saw this as an opportunity for his son to mature and learn how to break through some insecurities. Of course, every situation differs, but I encouraged her that when the issue involves letting go of our children, dads usually tend to be more objective. Men basically have been designed by God to protect, provide, and conquer. They echo the authority of God and, if you will, the adventurous side of his character. Women, on the other hand, are designed to bond, nest, and nurture. As such, women reflect the gentle, tender side of God. Their fierce devotion enables them to suffer great hardships on behalf of those they love. Their huge capacity for demonstrating compassion can be seen in many ways, but two places where these qualities are especially displayed are in birthing and nurturing.

Birthing

The starting point that makes any birthing possible is yieldedness. A spirit of receptivity must be present for birth to take place. Mary's response when she was told that she was going to conceive by the Holy Spirit is telling. She said, "I am the Lord's servant.... May it be to me as you have said" (Luke 1:38). She didn't resist, argue, or try to control. She didn't understand how it could happen, but that didn't keep her from saying "yes." Her relinquishment continued throughout the pregnancy. When faced with a skeptical community, an uncomfortable donkey ride, and even a no-vacancy inn, she wasn't distracted. She didn't complain, "How could you let me give birth in this stable when I'm doing your will?" Her commitment was unwavering. She had yielded to the will of God, and as a result, she birthed his glory.

As many women can readily testify, physical labor is not a fun experience. It is a painful, difficult process. I'll never forget our first childbirth classes when I was pregnant with Bethany. Chip took his job as coach very seriously, and he decided he was going to prepare me as much as possible. As we would practice the breathing exercises, he would squeeze my leg as hard as he could, even to the point of bringing tears to my eyes. Finally, he asked the childbirth instructor how effective she thought his little training drill was. With an all-knowing smile she responded, "Comparatively speaking, you're talking bee sting." How right she was! It's no wonder God gave the assurance in Genesis that the woman would be kept safe in childbirth. For many it still seems like a near-death experience.

A woman gives birth in the physical to demonstrate that all believers are marked to give birth spiritually. John 7:38 says, "Whoever believes in me as the Scripture says, streams of living water will flow from *within* him" (emphasis mine). In the King James Version, "within" is translated "out of his belly." The New American Standard interprets it as "innermost being or womb." Those who believe in Christ are to bring forth or *birth* streams of living waters. Paul knew this. He lamented to the Galatians, "My dear children for whom I am again in the pains of childbirth until Christ is formed in you" (Galatians 4:19).

Spiritual labor is difficult, just like physical labor. It requires travailing prayer and unrelenting persistence. When Jesus prayed in anguish at Gethsemane, he did it so you and I would have the opportunity to be *born again.* His "sweat was like drops of blood falling to the ground" (Luke 22:44). In a world that is increasingly characterized by a cut and run mentality, the spiritual laborers say *au contraire.* For them, there is no turning back. They deny their own comfort and ease to ensure that others make it safely through the birth canal. They will keep praying, keep giving, keep hoping, and keep *pushing* until the birth is completed.

Mothers are famous for their persistence. Remember the Canaanite woman who came to Jesus asking him to heal her demon-possessed daughter? Initially, Jesus ignored her. But she cried out all the more. His disciples, annoyed by her dogged determination, urged him to send her away. But she wasn't thwarted. She continued to ask, even after Jesus responded that he was sent only to help the people of Israel. When he told her it wasn't right to take the children's bread and toss it to their dogs, incredibly, the woman cried, "Then just give me the crumbs!" (Mark 7:25–30). Her daughter was healed because of her persistent intercession.

My dad didn't get saved until he was sixty-five years old. At my grandmother's funeral, he attributed his salvation to her persistent prayers through his many years of rebellion.

Not long ago, I read about a young man who was lost seven days in the Alps. The rescuers had given up hope of finding him, but his mother convinced them to go out one more time. That's when they found him—alive.

I remember when Kerry Collins, former quarterback at Penn State, led the Giants to the Super Bowl in 2001. Newspapers did a thorough job of chronicling his up and down bouts with alcoholism. Many were stunned at his drastic turn around when he was rehabilitated. But there was at least one who wasn't surprised…Roseanne Collins, Kerry's mother. Faith in her son during those tumultuous years never wavered.

A mother's persistence reflects God's persevering nature. We are given free will to give up on him, but he will not give up on us. Scripture says that even when we are unfaithful, he remains faithful because he cannot deny himself (2 Timothy 2:13). God intends to carry every birth to completion, no matter how inconvenient or troublesome the labor.

Nurturing

The second way mothers reflect the image of God is through nurturing. Mothering and nurturing are almost synonymous terms. The proper definition of nurture is to supply with nourishment; to educate; to further the development of; to foster (*Webster's New Collegiate Dictionary*).

Have you ever noticed how moms constantly want to make sure everyone gets enough to eat? Grandma would always say to us, "You need a little more meat on your bones." Summers of indulging in her cherry and raspberry pies inevitably resulted in more than "a little more meat"—more like a lot more fat. Nevertheless, she relentlessly pursued to make sure we weren't going to die from anorexia.

Mothers are always instructing and training their children. I home-schooled both of our children through eighth grade. Every excursion seemed to present itself, in my eyes, as a learning opportunity. One summer we spent our whole vacation at Gettysburg. That's right, eight days of ranger programs, wax museums, side trips to Harpers Ferry and Antietam, even an afternoon with "Abraham Lincoln." Bethany wrote five papers for school, and Josiah reenacted Pickett's Charge with his toy soldiers. No wonder our kids now prefer just to go to the beach for vacation.

Our femaleness enables us to nurture because we've been created with certain relational strengths. But I must say that everything I've learned about how to nurture has come from God, because he is a nurturer. When we, male or female, nurture, we reflect a part of God that communicates *you are cared for*. No one is exempt from needing to hear that message. Nurturing satisfies one of life's most basic necessities. Although it encompasses a lot of activities, comforting, sacrifice, and unconditional love embody three of the most important.

Comforting

God compares the way he comforts his people to that of a mother comforting her children. "As a mother comforts her child, so will I comfort you" (Isaiah 66:13). Scripture tells us that we are comforted so that we can comfort others with the comfort we ourselves have received (2 Corinthians 1:3–4). When someone is hurting, he or she may not be able to see God in the midst of the pain, so we serve as his representatives to help others know that they are not alone in the midst of the storm. Moms model this so well, and if they fall short of bringing comfort to their children, they feel miserable.

When my nephew, Sammy, entered first grade, he was not a happy camper. The third day of school his teacher approached my sister-in-law, Lisa, to inform her that he was not doing well. He was withdrawn, cried frequently in class, and wasn't eating his lunch (a definite sign of trouble). Clearly, he was having a hard time making the adjustment.

Since it took Lisa twenty-five minutes to drive Sammy to school, she seized the opportunity to try and prepare him for the day. On one particular occasion, he was very quiet, and she assumed he was starting to break through. But when they arrived at the school and she got out of her side of the car, Sammy immediately locked the door! Fortunately, Lisa had a key, so she unlocked the door; however, Sammy locked it again before she could get him out. After several repeats of this scenario, Lisa finally managed to thrust her body in the open door frame and rip him out of his seat. She tried to maneuver him across the yard. Have you ever tried to drag a kid who has his heels literally dug into the ground? Not a pretty sight.

The principal finally came to the rescue. She took them both to her office and calmly explained to Sammy that he had fifteen minutes left with his mom. At the end of the fifteen minutes, he could choose whether she or his mother would escort him to class. Well, Sammy went into full body-lock position. He had his arms and legs wrapped around Lisa so tightly that it would have taken half the staff to pry him loose. But at the end of the time, he went to class. His teacher held him close, prayed for him, and encouraged him to see that he was going to be all right. Then she had to do the same for Lisa! As Lisa was leaving the building, she could hold back no longer. She had burst into tears because of the anxiety her son was experiencing and her inability to comfort him. Now she was the one who needed to be comforted.

Sammy has progressed on to high school. He's adjusted quite well, but to this day, my tender-hearted sister-in-law gets a tear in her eye when she thinks of that first week of school.

Sometimes, comfort comes just in knowing that there is someone who's listening. I have a friend who calls from time to time just to unload. She's not really asking for counsel; she usually knows what to do. She just needs the comfort that comes from being heard. And that's fine with me, because I can't begin to count the number of times I have been allowed to pour out my heart to God.

When I was growing up, we used to sing a song:

> Now let us have a little talk with Jesus
> Let us tell him all about our troubles;
> He will hear our faintest cry and
> He will answer by and by...
> You will find a little talk with Jesus makes it right.[38]

Profound wisdom in that old country hymn. We have a God who is the ultimate comforter. He invites us to cast our cares on him because he cares for us (1 Peter 5:7). Whenever we take the time to listen, to encourage, or to lighten another's load, we display the comforting nature of our God.

Sacrifice

One of the most undeniable aspects of nurturing is its sacrificial nature. Nurturing cuts through our self-centeredness because it calls us to put another person's interests ahead of our own. From the beginning of natural motherhood, the sacrificial elements are obvious. Who, in their right mind would say "yes" if someone asked them to agree to the following for the next nine months: aching back; swollen ankles;

overriding nausea; inability to sleep through the night; emotional instability (you know, the kind that comes when your husband eats the last bit of ice cream that you were saving for yourself); a weight gain of thirty to sixty pounds, some of which you may never lose; and then to top it off, at the end of the nine months the most excruciating pain you've ever known. And that's just the entry into a whole new life of sacrifice! Who would agree to such a deal?

A mother!

"Be imitators of God, therefore, as dearly loved children and live a life of love, just as Christ loved us and gave himself up for us as a fragrant offering and sacrifice to God" (Ephesians 5:1–2). Like Christ, mothers would rather die themselves than see their children come to harm. It is notable that God asked Abraham, not Sarah, to offer Isaac as a sacrifice. I don't think Sarah could have done it. She most likely would have said, "Take my life instead." That's the nature of nurturing, maternal love. But it's only one part. When Abraham did offer Isaac, he, too, was reflecting an aspect of God's sacrificial nature. He was giving his only son—the one on whom all the promises of God depended. This parallels what the Father did when he gave his only Son. So an amazing thing happened on the cross: perfect maternal and perfect paternal love came together in sacrifice. Jesus said, "Don't take their lives; take mine instead." And the Father gave what is most dear to him for our sakes.

It is worth noting that man has a tendency to create God in his own image, hence, people view God through distorted lenses. They may see him as indifferent, too busy to be concerned about their troubles. Then when Christians do display selflessness, it is so rare that people may look upon them with suspicion. My friend, Sarah, invited an unbeliever in her neighborhood to a weekly Bible study in her home. But as they began meeting, the disruption of five small children in the basement became apparent. One of the teenage girls in our church volunteered to watch the children during the study so the adults would be less distracted. The initial reaction of the neighbor was that of suspicion. Why would Jazzmyn give up her time to serve someone she didn't know? Her worldview said there had to be a string attached somewhere.

Sacrificial lives will help redirect the impoverished eyes of a self-obsessed culture to the truth of God's sacrificial nature. His followers have the opportunity to reveal that he who "took up our infirmities and carried our sorrows," who "was pierced for our transgressions" and "crushed for our iniquities" (Isaiah 53:4–5) is the real deal.

Unconditional love

God chooses to forget our sins. Every day presents *new-every-morning mercies* (see Lamentations 3:22–23). Mothers echo that kind of resiliency. I remember when Bethany and Josiah were babies. No matter how frustrating their crying was through the night, it didn't make a dent in my love for them. One year in particular, when I homeschooled Josiah, it seemed like one or both of us ended up crying in class everyday. Yet it always amazed me how I was ready to try again the next day.

A few years after I was married, I became aware of how I had mistreated my mother during my teenage years. I went to her in tears of repentance, asking her to forgive me. You know how she responded? With a questioning look, she said, "I don't remember." Even when I tried to convince her of how rotten I was, she would have none of it.

A mother's love exemplifies the passage in 1 Peter 4:8 that exhorts us to "love each other deeply, because love covers a multitude of sins." The defining characteristic of unconditional love is just that: it places no requirements on its giving. It's not that flaws aren't seen or addressed. A mother may be more aware of her children's flaws than anyone. She simply loves in spite of them. It's just like God's love. His love isn't based on what we do or don't do. It looks beyond the surface and pulls out the good, even when we can't see it ourselves. Steady, consistent, and constant—unconditional love is never determined by how well we perform, nor is it withdrawn when we fail.

People who were not properly nurtured when they were young have difficulty comprehending God's unconditional love. For them, love must be earned; therefore, they tend to be bound to their performance, always fearing they'll make a mistake and not measure up. So what does God do? He puts his unconditional love for them in the hearts of those who are willing to be spiritual moms and dads. Such love breaks down, sometimes even bulldozes, through the walls of self-protection that have been erected, and a place of restoration is discovered.

Opposition

If mothers have a distinctive call to reflect the mark of compassion, it's no great surprise to discover forces at work that try to keep that compassion subdued. In the natural, what cuts off birth more than abortion or abandonment? Isaiah 49:15 says, "Can a mother forget the baby at her breast and have no compassion on the child she has born? Though she may forget, I will not forget you." Here, the Lord is using the illustration of a mother's attachment to her child to give a picture of his commitment to us. He compares himself with something that seems almost impossible—a mother forsaking her child—to help us understand the depth of his love. But today, mothers *are* forsaking their children. We all know the abortion statistics. And even more women today are simply abandoning their children in one form or another.

Similarly, in the spirit there are many places that should be bringing forth life but instead have stopped in midstream. Marriages, churches, and personal areas of growth that should be evidencing the mark of compassion are being aborted. The cost of "giving birth" for many has been deemed too high or too inconvenient.

Nurturing has been no less under attack. There is a strong, but subtle force prevailing in our society that is trying to make girls more like boys and stifle the nurturing instinct. This became quite apparent to me when Josiah was involved in wrestling. I was shocked to discover at his first match that little girls actually wrestled little boys. You might be thinking: *Where has she been*, but I was dumbfounded. Deeply troubled, I knew I had to do something. So I approached a woman who was there with her daughter and asked if her daughter was wrestling. "Yes," she answered with a proud smile.

I blurted out, "How could you let your daughter wrestle with little boys?"

Seemingly unfazed, she told me she saw nothing wrong with it, and besides, her daughter liked it. I was trying to convince her of the inappropriateness of it, when her husband, one of the coaches, came over. I asked him the same question, and he was even less receptive than his wife.

Two weeks later I went to another match. This time the girls were a bit older, around twelve years old. I was so disturbed that I began to cry. All I could think was: *What are these girls being trained to do?* The answer was clear: *They were being trained to use their bodies to win over boys at the expense of modesty.* The natural boundaries of touch were being violated. But their mothers saw pinning boys down to the mat as a way for their daughters to earn respect. I began talking about the situation with a neighbor who was there.

She remarked, "Yeah, it bothered me at first, but now I'm used to it."

I thought: *That's it. We're used to it. We've grown accustomed to women aborting their babies, to mothers dumping newborns in garbage cans, and to little girls exchanging their modesty to become like boys.*

But it doesn't have to remain this way. As Christians, we are called to bear the mark of compassion no matter how distorted the culture becomes. What we learn from moms—persistent, comforting, sacrificial, unconditional love—can cause us to lay tracks that will lead others to a finer picture of a heavenly Father's heart.

After God created Adam and Eve, he immediately told them why they were here. "God blessed them and said to them, 'Be fruitful and increase in number....'" (Genesis 1:28). In this day and age, when everyone is wondering about his or her purpose in life, isn't it interesting that the first recorded words of God to man reveal that purpose? That purpose, defined by the Creator, has never changed. Man is to be fruitful and multiply. Jesus makes it possible for us to fulfill that purpose by enabling us to reclaim our intimacy with God. But if there is something blocking our intimacy with him, we will remain barren; we will fail to bear the mark of fruitfulness.

DIGGING DEEPER

1. How have you reflected the principle of "spiritual birthing" in your life?
2. Name some things you've experienced that have required persistence—God's persistence with you and your persistence with someone else.
3. How have you seen God's nurturing care for you?

4. How have you demonstrated the comforting nature of God to others?
5. When was a time that God called you to sacrifice something for his sake?
6. Where have you experienced unconditional love? If you have not, how has that affected you?

CHAPTER 10

TOO MUCH BIRTH CONTROL
THE MARK OF FRUITFULNESS

There is a lot more in him than you guess, and a deal more than he has any idea of himself.

—*Gandalf*
(concerning Bilbo in *The Hobbit*)

SOME OF US are not unlike Bilbo Baggins in J. R. R. Tolkien's *The Hobbit*. We have a vast potential within us, but we hardly recognize the *what-could-be*. This is due, in part, to forces that want nothing more than to keep that potential latent and unproductive. Jesus said, "The thief comes only to steal, and kill and destroy. I have come that they may have life, and have it to the full" (John 10:10). Whether we realize it or not, Jesus came to mark our lives with abundance—brimming, overflowing, and bountiful. This abundant life is a result of our being united with him. But, as is the case in the natural, the bearing of fruit can be interrupted. The truth is that we are using too much "birth control" in our spiritual lives. These spiritual contraceptives serve to block the conception and development of the fruit of the Spirit we have been called to bear. This disruption can be likened to the thief that comes to steal, kill, and destroy. He wants to steal our destiny, kill our fruit, and destroy our intimacy with God—leaving behind the mark of barrenness, not fruitfulness.

Steal our Destiny

God loves people. As pointed out in the last chapter, his first great commission to Adam and Eve in the garden was to "be fruitful and increase in number" (Genesis 1:28). His commission to the early church was the same—be fruitful and multiply by "making disciples of all nations, baptizing them in the name of the Father, of the Son and of the Holy Spirit, and teaching them to obey everything I have commanded you" (Matthew 28:19–20). You see, God is in the *reproduction business*. He's the original "birthing place," the author of all life—natural and spiritual. He has planted in each of us seeds of life that pertain to our purpose and identity. But we have an enemy who wants to thwart the fulfillment of God's plan and literally steal our destinies. He will try any means to entice us toward a lesser goal than the one God has purposed for us.

In the book of Revelation we find an interesting passage that addresses the church in Thyatira: "You tolerate that woman Jezebel who calls herself a prophetess. By her teaching she misleads my servants into sexual immorality and the eating of food sacrificed to idols…. So I will cast her on a bed of suffering and I will make those who commit adultery with her suffer intensely unless they repent of her ways. *I will strike her children dead*" (Revelation 2:20–23, emphasis mine). The Jezebel referred to in this scripture is actually a spirit. The real Jezebel, the wife of Ahab (king of Israel), had been dead for hundreds of years. Responsible for bringing Baal worship to Israel, Jezebel caused the people to compromise their single-minded devotion to the Lord. This syncretism weakened them, resulting in their eventual downfall as a nation. The *spirit of Jezebel* was now seducing the early church with the same kind of compromise. By tolerating the worship of other gods, their consciences were becoming defiled, and the fruit that should have been produced wasn't even making it to the vine. Verse twenty-three says that her children will be struck dead. The fruit of joining with her resulted in death to the seeds of life that God had planted.

Israel…the early church…the present—the same principle applies to us today. When we compromise our love and faith in God for something lesser, we abort our destiny.

Let's not be ignorant of Satan's schemes. In order to steal our destiny he has to convince us that God's plan is either unrealistic or unattainable.

For example, you may be a mother who questions her effectiveness. Do you know God has ordained that you be a great mom? James Dobson says the self-doubt that mothers go through in our society is a cultural phenomenon. In a questionnaire distributed by Focus on the Family, 80% of the respondents were women, and their most frequent comment was, "I'm a failure as a mother." Dobson says that's just nonsense. Raising children is challenging, but God never intended it to be filled with guilt and self-doubt.[39] You see, Satan doesn't want us to raise godly children who may do damage to his kingdom. So he sends *Jezebel* to whisper that we're doing a terrible job in an attempt to discourage us to the point that our frustration may actually cause us to do poorly.

Perhaps you are venturing out in something new. The seeds in you are young and tender—therefore most vulnerable to the deception. The fruit hasn't begun to bud, and it's easy to think maybe it never will. It reminds me of going with my friend to the hospital when she was six months pregnant. All you could see on the outside was a protruding belly. It was hard to imagine that a whole life existed inside her. But the ultrasound revealed a complete little person with fingers and toes and hands and feet. The technician could see kidneys and heart chambers and even tell whether or not they were functioning properly. Today, Gracie (the baby) runs, laughs, and plays with all the other kids, but she was no less alive when she was "hidden in her mother's womb" than she is now.

I couldn't help but think of this as an analogy of spiritual life being formed in us. We can't see what's happening. We might feel kicks and pushes at times, but the actual life remains hidden. In times of discouragement and impatience, that spirit of Jezebel whispers, "Who do you think you are? You can't do anything or be anyone. There's nothing there." If we're not on guard, we succumb to the lies and allow our destiny to be snuffed out. But if we live by faith, not by sight, we will secure the destiny God has for us…and be marked with the fruitfulness he intends.

Kill our Fruit

Galatians 5:22–23 states, "But the fruit of the Spirit is love, joy, peace, patience, kindness, goodness, faithfulness, gentleness and self-control."

These fruits develop "naturally" as the believer yields him or herself to the work of the Holy Spirit. The significance of the evidence of the fruit can hardly be overestimated. Jesus said, "...I chose you and appointed you to go and bear fruit—fruit that will last. Then the Father will give you whatever you ask in my name" (John 15:16). Do you realize that you have been *appointed* to bear kindness...joy...self-control? Not only that, but you are also told that as you do, the Father will respond to your prayers. In light of the potency of such fruit production, is it any wonder that opposing forces would attempt to prevent their conception? Our fallen nature provides a seedbed for the enemy to formulate what I would call *spiritual condoms*, purposed to prohibit us from conceiving and bearing fruit. Let's look at the spiritual contraceptives at work to kill each fruit described in the aforementioned passage.

Love vs. Self-centeredness

Love is such an overriding characteristic of the Christian walk that Jesus said if we don't love, we really don't know God. We experience love in many different venues: a parent's love, a friend's love, a lover's love, love for country, love for music, love for country music (I hope you're smiling). Our capacity for love reaches far. But 1 John 4:10 defines love in a very interesting way: "This is love: not that *we* loved God, but that *he* loved us and sent his Son as an atoning sacrifice for our sins" (emphasis mine). Translated from the Greek word *agape,* this kind of love originates from God, not from our own needs or desires.

The spiritual contraceptive that hinders the manifestation of this love is self-centeredness. It presents the opposite of the love depicted in 1 Corinthians 13. An excerpt from The Message might describe it in the following way:

Self-centeredness easily gives up.
Self-centeredness cares more for self than others.
Self-centeredness wants what it doesn't have.
Self-centeredness likes to strut and has a swelled head.
Self-centeredness forces itself on others.
Self-centeredness expresses itself in "me first."

It's easy to see how self-centeredness keeps the fruit of love from being released. But it doesn't have to be this way. As we reject the condom of self-centeredness, *deny ourselves*, and follow Christ, the love of God will flow unrestrained.

Joy vs. Doubt and Worry

Doubt and worry are the contraceptives that block joy. When Jesus appeared to his disciples after the resurrection, Scripture says that "they still did not believe it because of joy and amazement…" (Luke 24:41). It was as if they were *afraid* to believe. The news was so astounding that they wouldn't let themselves experience joy, just in case it wasn't true. Doubt became a form of self-protection that kept the joy from being released.

How about us? Are we afraid to be joyful about good things in our lives in case it all comes crashing down? Do we operate under the "where's-the-other-foot-going-to-land" mentality? And if joy is hard to come by in good times, what about the seasons of struggle?

Joy erupts, no matter what the season, as we close the door on worry and enter the presence of the Lord. Author Dan Allender writes that "joy is a touch of sweet madness that comes when we sense God is closer to us than our own heartbeats." [40] One man who could have been consumed with worry but instead chose that "sweet madness" was Tony Snow, news commentator and press secretary to President George W. Bush. He died of colon cancer in the summer of 2008, at the age of 53. Tony wrote about his cancer in *Christianity Today*:

> Blessings arrive in unexpected packages—in my case, cancer. I don't know why I have cancer, and I don't much care. It is what it is—a plain and indisputable fact. Yet even while staring into a mirror darkly, great and stunning truths begin to take shape. Our maladies define a central feature of our existence: We are fallen. We are imperfect. Our bodies give out. But despite this—because of it—God offers the possibility of salvation and grace. We don't know how the narrative of our lives will end, but we get to choose how to use the interval between now and the moment we meet our Creator face-to-face….[41]

Tony's joy was contagious. It was said of him that no one could be in his presence and remain depressed, such was the strength of his optimism. When he left the Bush administration, not only the staff, but also the reporters (not known for their affection for press secretaries) lined up to give him a standing ovation. Tony's legacy stands as a powerful witness of one who refused to let doubt and worry block his joy in the greatest battle of his life.

Peace vs. Fear

Jesus warned his disciples that they would have trouble in the world, but in spite of it, they could have peace in him (John 16:33). He wanted them to understand that peace is not dependent upon external circumstances. In fact, Jesus had said earlier, "Do not suppose that I have come to bring peace to the earth. I did not come to bring peace, but a sword" (Matthew 10:34). An inevitable battle between good and evil erupts in Jesus' presence. The Prince of Peace exposes darkness, and unavoidable conflict ensues. Thus, we can not release the fruit of peace until we have first engaged in war to get it. And the first clash requires us to face our fears. Fear is the contraceptive that blocks peace.

The fall of man introduced fear into a world that had known no fear. Adam and Eve hid themselves from God's presence because they were afraid—they knew their sin was uncovered. Fear of exposure has followed fallen man since the garden, as have our futile attempts to cover ourselves. We fear intimacy. We fear failure. We fear success. We fear taking responsibility. We fear being vulnerable. We fear death. (My students would add Public Speaking to the list). As long as these fears remain in us, we will never know true peace. So we must go to war and let the light of Christ touch those fear-ridden areas that have remained in hiding.

As believers, we must not avoid the necessary battles that bring true and lasting resolution. It is not "more Christian" to leave well enough alone rather than confront difficult issues. I find inspiration for the fight from British Prime Minister Winston Churchill. In World War II, Churchill warned the world that anything less than a full assault against the enemy would result in failure. He knew the easier road of appeasement would ultimately lead to defeat, and he challenged his countrymen to fully embrace the ensuing conflict. He said:

> We have nothing to offer but blood, toil, tears, and sweat. We have before us an ordeal of the most grievous kind.... We have before us many many months of struggle and suffering. Our policy—to war with all our might and the strength God has given us; our aim—victory, for without victory there is no survival.[42]

Let's not be afraid to take off the condom of fear—even if it means going to war to achieve peace.

Patience vs. Lust

Patience means being able to wait. The contraceptive that prohibits it from being produced is lust. Consider lust as *anything* we have to have, and have now. It can range from sex, to food, to material goods of all kinds. In a fast-paced society such as ours, patience is hard to cultivate. Waiting makes us feel like we're wasting our time. We want to get where we're going as quickly as possible, so we abhor traffic or waiting in line. Our impatience is catered to by drive-thru fast food restaurants, banks, and photo marts. We like microwaves. We crave high-speed internet. We lust for immediate gratification and instant success. And we probably think we deserve it.

I think of the story of Achan, recorded in Joshua 7. When Israel defeated Jericho, the people were told *not* to take any plunder for themselves. It was their first battle, and they were to honor God by offering all the spoils to him. But Achan couldn't wait. If he could just have held off until the next battle, he would have gotten all the spoils he wanted, but his lust provoked him to grab ahead of time. His disobedience resulted in not only his death, but also the death of his family. (Lust always hurts more than just the one lusting). Maybe Achan didn't trust that God would be fair or faithful, so he felt he had to *do it his way.* But God's intention was not to deprive Israel; he gave them the victory in the first place. He had a bigger picture. Not only did he want them to win, but also he wanted to train them *how* to win. It was essential that they learned to revere God first, above the many victories they would be experiencing in the days to come. There is typically a broader perspective to God's timing than what we see.

Over the years I've realized that there has been almost nothing of significance I've longed for that has happened *when* I wanted it to happen. Yet, it was in those waiting times that God received my most undivided attention, taught me to trust, and enabled me to get rid of the contraceptive of lust.

Kindness vs. Complacency

I think of kindness as a highly-underrated fruit. It seems to sometimes get camouflaged in other virtues, but in reality, it packs a powerful punch. God's kindness leads us to repentance (Romans 2:4). Kind words have the ability to cheer up anxious hearts (Proverbs 12:25). Acts of kindness to the poor bring honor to the Lord (Proverbs 14:31). Kindness displays an interest in another's welfare. We see it evidenced in deeds that go beyond the norm or what is expected. People who are kind have a way of making us feel we're important to them. Although kindness may be expressed in *random acts,* kindness doesn't just happen. It requires effort. Thus, the contraceptive that blocks kindness is complacency. We don't want to put forth the extra work for someone else's benefit.

One of the kindest men I've ever known was Ernst Krebs, a man who would never be categorized as complacent. Ernst was a retired evangelist whose home Chip and I visited while traveling in Switzerland. Since retiring, Ernst had spent his days farming and raising sheep. His neighbor, who knew nothing about sheep, became very disturbed when he saw Ernst docking the sheep's tails. He thought Ernst was being cruel and insisted that he stop such an inhumane practice. Ernst, not wanting to offend this neighbor, decided to let his sheep's tails grow in deference to him. To ensure that his sheep not get diseased from stool that could now get trapped in their tails, Ernst would have to undergo the laborious task of cleaning them regularly. But to Ernst, it was worth it if it was a way to demonstrate the kindness and love of Christ.

Acts of kindness are powerful, but they will never be cultivated if we yield to complacency. I think of my friend Ann, who often begins her prayers with a deep sense of gratitude that God would chose to use her to carry out one of his assignments. Those assignments might include inviting people to dinner every Tuesday night, hosting exchange students, or spending hours to refurbish the classroom where she works to make it special for the children. She bears choice fruit because she is willing to go the extra mile.

Goodness vs. Pride

In Matthew 19:17, a rich young ruler asked Jesus what good thing he had to do to inherit eternal life. Jesus responded by saying that there was only one who was good, and that was God. He said this to dispel the ruler from the notion that our goodness or good works could get us to heaven. Jesus wanted him—and us—to know that there is no true goodness apart from God. The contraceptive that blocks that true goodness is pride. Pride beckons us to rest on our own good deeds and think that what we do is *good enough*.

When I tell my son, Josiah, he's done a "good job," what I'm usually saying is that he's obeyed what I told him to do. When it's not a good job, it's because he's decided what's good enough. His pride in determining what is good by his standards (rather than mine) inevitably leads him to selective obedience. It reminds me of the serpent's temptation to Eve. Rather than letting God tell her what was good (or evil), she chose to determine it herself by eating from the tree of the knowledge of good and evil, which she was told not to do. She thought it would be a *good* thing, even making her like God. But this pride led to destruction (Genesis 3).

Many people engage in good activities, outside of the church and within. But we run the danger of fostering pride in our own accomplishments if these "good" things are not directed by God. As we look over the good *we* have done, we may even evaluate ourselves as "good," and before we know it, we reek of self-righteousness. The true goodness that flows from God is blocked. If we want goodness to pour from us, we will have to get rid of any notion that *we* are good. The degree that goodness emanates from us reflects the extent that the contraceptive of pride has been removed.

Faithfulness vs. Idolatry

Idolatry is the spiritual condom that blocks faithfulness. What do you daydream about? What do you imagine? Worshiping idols begins with envisioning something or someone other than God to bring fulfillment. It slowly develops into our actively pursuing and trusting another one or thing for our deliverance. That's what happened to Israel. Time and time again, Israel, rather than trusting God, turned to other nations for rescue. Isaiah lamented, "Woe to those who go down to Egypt for help, who rely on horses, who trust in the multitude of their chariots and in the great strength of their horsemen, but do not look to the Holy One of Israel, or seek help from the Lord" (Isaiah 31:1). Once Israel began relying on the horses and chariots of Egypt, it wasn't long before they were worshiping Egypt's gods. They had ceased being faithful to the Lord.

I find it fascinating that Israel was in fact turning to the nation that had once enslaved them. But what do we do when we get tired of waiting on God? When we're scared that he's not going to be there *this time*, where do we look for help? When our vision of God's faithfulness is occluded, what do we imagine? How often do we return to our old ways and means of dealing with issues…the Egypt from which we were delivered? I'm afraid that all too often, rather than envisioning God rescuing us, we see ourselves working it out. *We* become the idol that replaces God. We rely on the horses of our minds, the chariots of our emotions, and the strength of our manipulation. Slowly but surely our actions once again revert to what *we* want, what *we* desire. We end up bowing down to the mirror, loving ourselves far too much to worship anyone else.

We must always be on guard so as not to let any idol replace our faithfulness to the Lord. "Many a man claims to have unfailing love, but a faithful man who can find?" (Proverbs 20:6). The fruit of faithfulness is a rare commodity, one the world very much needs to taste.

Gentleness vs. Control

The drive to be in control is the contraceptive that blocks gentleness. Controlling people resist gentleness because it makes them feel too vulnerable. They fear they might be taken advantage of if they present a "soft" side. Or they're so used to getting things accomplished by their take-charge mentality that they believe any variation from their control will result in nothing getting done, or at least not in the way they want. They carry a distorted image of *gentle* people, whom they view as weak-kneed wusses who are afraid to take a stand. But this contradicts the scriptural view of gentleness. Proverbs 15:1 says, "A gentle answer turns away wrath," and Proverbs 25:15 says, "...a gentle tongue can break a bone." Gentleness sounds pretty strong to me.

One of the few places in Scripture where something is specifically designated as being of "great worth" to God is found in 1 Peter 3: 4. In referring to how wives should relate to their husbands, Peter lauds the "unfading beauty" of a woman's "*gentle* and quiet spirit" as being of "*great worth* in God's sight" (emphasis mine). But the relationship between husbands and wives all too often turns into a contest, with each one clamoring to be the one in control. Words become vindictive rather than affirming. Aggression replaces gentleness. Rather than allowing their differences to *complete* one another as God intended, they *compete* with each other. What a difference an "*I*" makes!

Lavanna Waller was a member of my church when I was growing up. Her husband was mean, gruff, and unsaved. But she always met his roughness with gentleness. Mrs. Waller was at church every time the doors were opened. She shouted and cried and laughed, always giving glory to God, never ceasing to pray for her husband's salvation. She was well into her seventies when he died, and on his deathbed, he at long last embraced Christ. There is no doubt in my mind that he was "won over" by the "unfading beauty" of her "gentle and quiet spirit."

I urge you, whether male or female, not to fall into the control trap and keep the gentleness of the Lord at bay. Give up whatever rights to control you think you have, and let the gentle Spirit of Christ be unconfined. Ironically, the fruit of gentleness has a far greater influence than all our puny attempts at control.

Self-control vs. Self-indulgence

Although controlling others diminishes the reflection of Christ, this is not the case when we are dealing with ourselves. The ability to exercise self-control dictates our future impact perhaps more than any other fruit. Without self-control there is no discipline, and without discipline, there can be no success.

The obvious contraceptive that hinders self-control is self-indulgence. We don't stop when we should. We eat too much, talk too much, and play too much. Self-indulgence indicates a lack of vision. Proverbs 29:18 says, "Where there is no revelation, the people cast off restraint..." If there's nothing to anticipate, why go through the rigorous discipline of self-denial?

You may be familiar with the Stanford Marshmallow Study that was conducted in the 1970s.[43] A group of four-year-olds were placed in a room and presented with a marshmallow. They were told that they could either eat the marshmallow immediately, or if they waited until the researcher returned from a brief errand, they could have two. Follow-up on these same students thirteen years later revealed interesting results. The children who had denied their immediate desire for the marshmallow and waited so they could have two, went on to perform significantly better throughout their schooling and were better socially adjusted. Those who had been unable to delay immediate gratification were found to be insecure and unhappy. Overall, they continued to lack the capacity to say "no" to something desirable today for the sake of something better tomorrow.

God doesn't want our fruitfulness to be restrained by the contraceptive of self-indulgence. He wants to train us to exercise self-control when the realization of our goals and dreams requires waiting. His vision for us doesn't include running frantically from project to project, church to church, and relationship to relationship in vain attempts to find a shortcut to fulfillment.

Destroy our Intimacy

Perhaps the greatest contraceptive of all is caused by the failure to be intimate. Without intimacy in the natural, there is definitely no conception. Similarly, unless we experience an intimate relationship with God, we will not conceive and bear fruit. Wounds and hurts from our past can keep us from moving into that level of relationship. Rather than trusting God and allowing ourselves to be vulnerable before him, we protect ourselves. Protecting ourselves makes us feel safer. That's the point. Pregnancy is avoided when condoms provide "safe sex." Likewise, when we protect ourselves from intimacy with God, the result is barrenness.

God desires us to see him as our protector. He wants us to experience being with him as being in the safest place imaginable. Jesus revealed this when he prayed in John 17:12–17: "While I was with them, I protected them and kept them safe by that name you gave me…. My prayer is that you protect them from the evil one." Then, he goes on to say, "Sanctify them by the truth." The truth can make us feel very vulnerable. It strips away all our masks and defenses. It tears down our walls of self-protection that have been so carefully crafted. But in the exposure, it purifies what lies within. Walking in the truth opens the door for us to recognize Jesus as a safe Savior. We become less guarded, and intimacy flourishes.

So, how do we cultivate this kind of intimacy? For starters, consider these suggestions. First, don't hold back. Intimacy involves shared confidences between two people, and that's the way it is between God and us. Tell God what you're thinking and feeling. Talk to him all the time, not just in morning devotions or nighttime prayers. Tell him when you're being tempted and when you need help to stand. If something delights you, tell him, and thank him for it. Tell him about your frustrations. Tell him if you blew it and yelled at the kids. Tell him how touched you were when a friend called just to check on you. Tell him how honored you were when he used you in a specific way. Pause often throughout the day just to whisper, "Jesus I love you." Let your communication with God be like breathing. Assume he wants a more intimate relationship with you. The one who numbers the hairs on your head (Luke 12:7) is interested in every aspect of your life.

Second, listen to music that elicits a response of love and confidence in God. Agree with lyrics that have been penned to evoke abandoned devotion. On my morning walks, I often find myself singing, "Thou my best thought by day or by night…" or "There is none like you. No one else can touch my heart like you do…" Expressing to God our love for him actually increases our affection. God-focused lyrics also fortify our faith.

Modern-day hymnist Keith Getty, writer of "In Christ Alone," speaks of the importance of singing music that retells the story of redemption. Songs that direct us to the cross remind us of Jesus' sacrifice and draw us to him in ways other things fail to do.

A Great Potential

A story told by Dr. Frederick Loomis crystallizes, for me, the importance of recognizing the potential in every human life. When Loomis first began practicing obstetrics, a young pregnant woman came into his office. It was soon discovered that her baby was in breech position, necessitating that he reach into the womb and pull the baby out, feet-first, during delivery. As the baby was being born, he reached for the tiny feet, only to discover that the entire thigh on one leg, from the hip to the knee, was missing. At that moment he struggled with what he described as the greatest battle of his life—whether to proceed with the delivery, knowing the tremendous hardship it would have on the family, or simply to delay the birth, allowing the baby to die, with no one ever knowing what he had done. He quickly decided he wouldn't bring the unnecessary burden of a handicapped child to this family. But a sudden, vigorous movement of strength coming from the infant disarmed his rationalization. He delivered the baby, chastising himself for not having the courage to prevent the ensuing sorrow. He eventually lost all contact with the family.

Fast forward seventeen years. It was the hospital Christmas party. On the stage of the auditorium were three lovely musicians who would be performing for the program. The doctor was particularly drawn to the young woman playing the harp. She played with such extraordinary grace and talent that he was moved to tears. After the program was finished, a woman came running up to him. He didn't recognize her, but she, full of pride and exuberance, knew him. "Did you see her?" the woman exclaimed. "That was my daughter playing the harp, the one with the bad leg you delivered seventeen years ago. She is becoming one of the world's greatest harpists."[44]

Don't abort the life God is birthing in you. No matter how distorted or impaired you think your life has been, God's redemptive work is greater. Don't let contraceptives steal, kill, and destroy your fruit. You have a destiny to fulfill. God desires to have an intimate relationship with you that is marked with fruitfulness—fruitfulness for which a hurting world is waiting.

I hope it's clear that how we respond to God—his conviction, his leading, his love—determines the mark of fruitfulness in our lives. Our ability to respond, our *response-ability*, as some have coined it, rests on recognizing the voice calling us. Hearing God poses as a fundamental requisite for those who want to leave tracks that will last…tracks honed by the mark of listening.

DIGGING DEEPER

1. Do you recognize ways Satan has tried to "steal your destiny"?
2. Name some areas in your life where you have seen love released as a result of self-denial.
3. Are there times when doubt and worry have blocked your joy? How have you overcome?
4. When was a time you had to "go to war" in order to get peace?
5. When is it hardest for you to wait?
6. Describe a time when you have been affected by someone's kindness toward you.
7. Are there "good things" you've had to lay on the altar? Explain the outcome.
8. Where are you most likely to look for help, if not in the Lord?
9. Where is an area you might need to give up control in order to bear the fruit of gentleness?
10. What can you do to cultivate greater intimacy with the Lord?

CHAPTER 11

HEARING GOD 101
THE MARK OF LISTENING

He is there, and he is not silent.

—Francis Schaeffer

WHEN MY MOM was still living in southern Ohio, her telephone number was one digit off the number of the unemployment office, so she invariably received mistaken calls. It was so consistent that she finally put the following message on her answering machine: "Hello, this is Mandy, *not* the unemployment office. I'm either shopping, bowling, or playing golf." But what people *hear* is often determined by what they *think they will hear.* One time she came home and heard a disgruntled caller complain, "No wonder they don't get any work done around there!"

In Matthew 4:4, Jesus said that man lives "on every word that comes from the mouth of God." God speaks, but our spiritual sustenance depends upon whether or not we hear what he says. We can be like the people on Mom's answering machine who didn't bother listening because they thought they already knew what was being said, or we can recognize our need for daily manna and open our ears. Whether we have been believers for a number of years or have recently come into the faith, hearing God comprises one of the most crucial aspects of our Christianity if we want to leave indelible tracks.

But how *do* we hear God? What if we can't hear? What about those people who say God told them to kill someone? What effect does hearing God have on us? What effect does it have on our ministry? I believe an understanding of the basic elements involved in hearing God will help answer some of these questions as well as assist us in acquiring the mark of listening.

Element 1: Hearing God Must Be Recognized as Vital to Everyone Who Wants to Live Fully in Christ.

One of the prerequisites for faith is the ability to hear God. The Bible says that "faith cometh by hearing and hearing by the Word of God" (Romans 10:17 KJV). Since faith lays the foundation for our whole spiritual life, it would be hard to overestimate the importance of hearing God's Word. Hearing God is not reserved for preachers and prophets. No less than fifteen times, the Scripture admonishes "those who have ears to hear." If we "have ears," we qualify to have God speak to us. God is a communicating God. Jesus himself is referred to as the "Word" (John 1:1). He wants to speak to all of us, all the time. Even his silence can speak volumes.

Yet, for some, the notion of hearing God remains a vague concept. Why? Because Satan knows, probably better than we do, the significance of hearing God. Being the great deceiver, he will always try to distort God's Word and bring confusion to our minds. It's a strategy he has used since the fall of the human race. Look at Genesis 3:1: "Now the serpent was more crafty than any of the wild animals the Lord God had made. He said to the woman, 'Did God really say you must not eat from any tree in the garden?'" He put a question in her mind that caused her to doubt what God had said. After she was open to doubt, he redefined the Lord's words, assuring her that she "will not surely die" (verse 4). We know what happened as a result.

Devoid of original creativity, Satan can only take a seed of truth that already exists and twist and pervert it until it is no longer recognizable. Because we have inherited Adam and Eve's fallen nature, we know that we, too, are targeted for his deception. We hear stories about people or know people who have obviously been deceived into thinking they heard

God when they clearly didn't. I remember a woman in Florida who said God told her she was going to marry a doctor. The problem—she was married to someone else. So she divorced her husband in order to do what *God said.* Cultish leaders like Jim Jones and David Koresh convince their followers that God has spoken to them. Then they lead their devotees into destruction. Patients in mental institutions claim a "voice" has told them they are Jesus Christ. People have justified all kinds of selfish behavior and caused much pain by labeling their actions as "the Lord told me to do it."

In most of these situations the word people hear doesn't match up with what God has already spoken in the written Word. In fact, one sure indication that we're not hearing God is when what we are hearing differs from what has been recorded in the Scriptures. If it contradicts what the Bible says, it cannot be from God. And we must never place what we think God is saying to us in specific situations on an equal plane with the inspired written Word.

Nevertheless, situations like this can make us skittish as we approach hearing God. We don't want to be deceived, nor do we want to misrepresent God in any way. So we can tend to back off and "play it safe." We say, "Let the pastor or priest tell me about what God says in general, but when it comes to personal decisions or dilemmas, I'll rely on my own thinking to make the best choices I can."

Now, just because some people have abused the privilege of hearing God by letting themselves be deceived, that's no excuse for us to go about listening in a half-hearted manner. That, too, is walking in deception. In 2 Thessalonians 2:10–11 it says, "They perish because they refused to love the truth and so be saved. For this reason God sends them a powerful delusion so that they will believe the lie…." Those who are deceived are those who love the lie more than the truth. If we remain steadfast in loving the truth, God will not let us be deceived. Throughout our years in ministry, we have encountered numerous heretical teachings that people have supposedly *heard* from God. But God has always diverted us from the deception, honoring our commitment to love the truth and actively seek it.

Element 2: Hearing God Is Something We Learn How To Do Progressively.

It's erroneous to think that there are two categories of people: those who hear God and those who don't. Those who hear more, hear more not necessarily because God speaks to them with greater frequency, but because they develop the ability to hear what God is saying. Just as we learn to communicate with other people, so we learn to commune with God. We do this primarily through reading the Scriptures, spending time in prayer, and walking in obedience.

If we don't have a regular pattern of reading the Bible, we can't expect to grow in hearing God. Every morning I get up early so I can spend time alone with the Lord. I come with a notebook, pen, Bible, and devotional book of some kind. I begin by writing down any thoughts or impressions that come to mind. Sometimes I express gratitude for the coming day or for something that occurred the day before. Then I read two different passages in the Bible—either something from the New Testament or Old and a Psalm or Proverb. I write down the Scripture reference and ask God how the passage applies. If I don't hear anything in particular, I at least write a summary of the selection. Then I read from whatever devotional book I'm using that year, and I again write down any specific impressions I receive. This daily exercise gives me a sense of accountability to help me listen. After that, I pray, often using what I've read as a starting point for my prayers. This pattern may not work for you. But I would encourage you to find some kind of pattern that does. One of the most surprising observations I've had over the years is how many Christians struggle with maintaining a consistent devotional life. Sadly, Satan has been far too effective in sabotaging our view of the necessity of daily communion with the Lord.

Obedience to what we do hear amplifies our perception. James warned, "Do not merely listen to the word, and so deceive yourselves. Do what it says" (1:22). As we respond in a practical way to a directive, our sensitivity to his voice is heightened. It's what I call "following the nudges." We send flowers to a friend. We invite someone to dinner. We make a phone call. We sense a hesitation in allowing our child to participate in a certain event. Do we mishear at times? Certainly. Do we make mistakes? Of course. But as we seek to obey in response to the nudging, we will develop a greater familiarity with his voice.

Element 3: Examine the Hindrances and Get Rid of Them.

A number of hindrances get in the way of our hearing God, but busyness may be the most prevalent one for many of us. When our lifestyles becomes so hurried that we fail to take the time to stop and listen, we forfeit a precious opportunity. Sometimes my days feel like a nine month pregnancy—stretched to full capacity. When communion with the Lord is not the priority, all the telltale signs that accompany busyness—impatience with other people, intolerance for interruptions, methodically going through the motions—surface. We simply cannot afford to crowd out communication with God and succumb to louder voices. Being busy is not a bad thing, but being too busy reveals an obsession to fill up our time. Our lives become like sentences with no commas. To break through, we must intentionally do the opposite of what we feel: pause and get quiet before the Lord. Responding to the exhortation to "Be still and know that I am God" (Psalm 46:10) assures us that the mark of listening is being honed.

A second hindrance lies in failing to recognize God's voice when he does speak. Remember the story of Samuel? As a young boy, he served in the temple under Eli the priest. One night when Samuel was sleeping, he heard a voice calling his name. Supposing it was Eli, he went to him to see what he wanted. Eli told him he hadn't called. This happened a second, then a third time. Finally, Eli realized it must be the Lord calling Samuel. The Bible says that in "those days the word of the Lord was rare" (1 Samuel 3:1). Because hearing God was such an infrequent occurrence, Eli missed it when he did speak. We must not let ourselves get accustomed to not expecting God to speak to us. I believe he probably speaks more than we realize. But if we're not anticipating his voice, we're not positioning ourselves to hear.

Recently a number of people from our church were planning to go on a short-term mission trip to Nicaragua. Chip and I felt the Lord wanted Josiah to participate, but we also believed it was important for him to hear God if, in fact, this was a divine directive. So Josiah prayed, but he continued to report that he didn't have an answer. We were getting down to the wire. He had to make a commitment in the next few days, but he was still hearing nothing. Then at his youth meeting he asked his youth leader, Jim, to pray with him specifically for an answer. When they finished praying, Jim told him, "I believe God is going to clearly speak to you on the way home tonight." Now, our church is about seven minutes from our house, so if God was going to speak there would only be a small window of opportunity. But about half way home, Josiah happened to spot a landscaping truck parked by the road. Painted on its side was an acronym for its business...Y.E.S. in big, bold letters. Josiah *knew* God had given him his answer. Some might call it a coincidence, but I believe God wanted to teach a young boy about the importance of expecting to hear his voice.

Another hindrance in developing listening skills lies in our need to understand everything before we acknowledge his voice. In reality, we rarely catch the full picture. The Scripture says that we *know in part* (1 Corinthians 13:9). If we want to grow in hearing, we must be willing to let go of our demand to know why before we respond. If the Lord prompts us to do something and we refuse because we don't see how it would work, our experience of hearing God will be short-circuited. Parents give their children directives all the time without the children having a full understanding of why. We expect them to obey because they *trust* us, not because they have found a reason that sounds good to them. God expects no less. As we respond to the part that we do hear, and leave the rest to God, more will be added.

Emotions and misperceptions are further hindrances that act as static in the airways, masking over the voice of the Lord. Our anger or anxiety can scream so loudly that every other sound is muffled. Depression deafens perhaps more than any other emotion we experience. Or sometimes we wrongly think we could hear better if our circumstances were different. But God's voice is not stifled by our circumstances. He has an amazing way of speaking *through* our situations, not in spite of them. He speaks to mothers as they nurse their babies; he speaks to prisoners locked in solitary confinement; he speaks to executives in their boardrooms; he speaks to soldiers on the front line; he speaks to college students; he speaks to Wal-Mart greeters. Psalm 29 tells us the voice of the Lord covers the waters, shakes the desert, and strips the forests. There is no place on earth or heaven where his voice cannot penetrate. Don't let emotional distress or "unlikely" circumstances keep you from listening.

A final hindrance may be found in simple rebellion. We don't hear because we really don't want to hear. We're afraid God might tell us to do something we don't desire to do. And if we haven't heard, we think we won't be held accountable. I remember once when a friend of ours was trying to decide whether or not to go into business. He knew it was something he wanted to do, and as he explained how he was seeking the Lord about it, he put his hands over his ears and said, "I'm listening, God." Some of us show even more sophistication than this in our resistance to hearing. We go straight for the moldable type ear plugs that form to our ear canal and block out *everything*. Or we play the selective listening game—give me the burger, but hold the lettuce and tomatoes, please. It's a vain attempt to live in both worlds. We add our own agenda to what God has said, and it corrupts it all. Scripture gives a clear description of this kind of "hearing": "You will be ever hearing but never understanding…for this people's heart has become calloused; they hardly hear with their ears…" (Matthew 13:14–15). A rebellious, calloused heart refuses to hear the voice of the Lord.

Element 4: When You Can't Hear, Go Back To the Last Thing You Did Hear and Hold on Tenaciously.

When your inability to hear God is not due to rebellion or any of the other hindrances we've discussed, recall the last thing you believe he said and cling to it. I like the example in Lewis' *The Silver Chair.* Aslan sends the children to find Prince Rillian, who has been captured by the Emerald Witch. He gives them three signs to help them find the path that leads to the prince. He says, "Here on the mountain, the air is clear and your mind is clear; as you drop down into Narnia, the air will thicken. Take great care that it does not confuse your mind. And the Signs which you have learned here will not look at all as you expect them to look, when you meet them there. That is why it is so important to know them by heart and pay no attention to appearances. Remember the Signs and believe the Signs. Nothing else matters."[45] Lewis was illustrating how circumstances can greatly alter our perception of things. If God has spoken to us, we must remain firm and not waver in what he has said, even when it seems like the opposite is happening.

My sister-in-law, Lisa, had been diagnosed with breast cancer for the third time. While receiving heavy doses of chemo therapy in preparation for a bone marrow transplant, she developed thrush, a common side effect from the drugs. The sores in her throat and mouth were so painful that she couldn't eat and could barely drink. She waned weaker and weaker. Around ten on a Saturday night, my brother, Marty, called to ask for prayer because he didn't know what else to do. He specifically asked us to pray for Lisa to get stronger and also for him to have wisdom. As I hung up the phone, anxiety and fear engulfed me. Our friends Diane and Sarah were visiting, and they joined us in praying for the situation.

As Diane began to pray, she recalled something I had stated previously—that I felt the Lord wanted us to believe for miracles in the coming year. When Diane reiterated that word in her prayer and applied it to Lisa's situation, my faith began to be rejuvenated. It was like watering a wilting plant and watching it spring back to life. The fear and anxiety lifted as I stood upon what the Lord was causing us to remember and appropriate. By the time we finished praying, I was confident that God was taking care of Lisa.

The next day my brother phoned and said that not long after talking to me, he called a lady in their church who was a nurse. She came immediately and checked Lisa's blood. She discovered that Lisa's blood sugar was extremely low, and she instructed Marty to get her some Gatorade. Within twenty minutes, Lisa began to revive. We later found out that she had been dangerously close to slipping into a coma. God had answered our prayers. He had given Marty the wisdom we had asked for, and he had strengthened Lisa. But he had also taught me a vital lesson about the importance of holding on to the things he has spoken. As we began to pray, I couldn't hear what the Lord was saying, but I could hold on to something he had said before and was clearly recalling to my mind.

Element 5: Hearing God Is the Primary Means By Which We Develop Intimacy with God.

Just as true intimacy between two people expands through communication, so our communication with God intensifies and strengthens our relationship with him. Hymn writer Fanny Crosby wrote, "I am Thine, O Lord; I have *heard* Thy voice, and it told Thy love to me…"[46] What was it that convinced Fanny Crosby that she belonged to God? According to this hymn, she heard his voice, and his voice spoke of his love for her.

In John 10:4–5, Jesus describes the bond between a shepherd and his sheep: "…his sheep follow him because they know his voice. But they will never follow a stranger; in fact, they will run away from him because they do not recognize a stranger's voice." The reason the sheep follow their shepherd is because they recognize his voice. Jesus depicts his relationship with us in similar fashion: "My sheep listen to my voice; I know them, and they follow me" (John 10:27). In this verse, Jesus weaves together listening, knowing, and following. As we listen to him speak to us on a personal level, we realize he knows us. And because he knows us, we trust him enough to follow him.

If I were to get a phone call right now and an unidentifiable voice told me to get in my car and drive two hours to the Philadelphia airport, I would be curious at such a request, but I doubt that I would go. If I recognized the voice as being somewhat familiar, maybe that of a minor acquaintance, I might consider it a bit more, but I would still be reluctant to drop everything and go. However, if the call came from someone who knew me, like my husband, and he said, "Becky, I know you're busy right now, but it's important that you stop working on your book, hop in the car, and drive immediately to the Philadelphia airport," I would go. I wouldn't even have to know the reason why (although I probably would ask). My response would be based on knowing the *voice* and knowing the *voice* knew me.

The awareness that there is Someone who knows us, *really knows* us, and still calls us his own encompasses one of the most profound experiences in life. Jesus wants you to know that he knows all about you—the good, the bad, and the ugly—yet he never ceases in wanting you to be his own. And the way we discover this comes through hearing him. God wants to speak to each of us in a personal way so we will come. The Bible looks like a form letter to those who don't know the voice of the Lord. But those who know the author·find it to be the source of a deep, ongoing relationship.

Element 6: Hearing God Impacts the World

Not only are we enriched personally by hearing God, but also the effects of listening to him reach far beyond ourselves. If we desire to leave our mark on the world, only those things initiated by God will have an eternal impact. Each man's works will be tested by fire. If the works we have done on the earth have been initiated by the Word of God, they will pass the test. But works that are self-initiated will be consumed. Throughout my years as a Christian, God has demonstrated the effects of listening to his voice in many ways. Let me share a couple of examples...

At times God's directives can be somewhat humorous, like when our church needed a new piano. The strings were breaking on a regular basis; on one occasion, five popped at the same time! We had to call the piano tuner in so often that it seemed like we must be putting her children through college. Chip had encouraged Diane, our keyboard player, to start looking for a new piano. She found a digital one that would have the added advantage of not going in and out of tune with fluctuating heat patterns. It was a bit expensive, so Chip asked God to speak to him as to whether or not he should pursue it. As he was driving down the road he prayed, "Lord, please make it clear to me." Right then, he looked up and saw a billboard on the road that said in big, bold letters, "YOU CAN'T AFFORD IT." Although the sign was referring to drunk driving, Chip was convinced that God had spoken to him about the piano. He knew he was to wait. A month later I happened to see a coupon in the paper advertising that very same piano, now on sale at a significantly reduced price.

The piano incident impacted not only our music ministry, but it also served as an example to the whole church about the importance of hearing God. A far greater effect was realized through listening and waiting than if we had just gone out and purchased a piano.

Another example of the effect of hearing God occurred during the summer a young married couple lived in our home. Kevin and Laura had hopes of buying their first house with the intention of serving in campus ministry at a local university. Houses near most college campuses usually run higher than in other places. Even though they knew they were facing an uphill battle because of their limited funds, Kevin and Laura prayed. Then one day, Chip received a call from a Christian family living near the campus. They were moving and wanted to sell their house to someone who had a heart for student ministry. They weren't interested in making a lot of money, and they were selling it for far less than they could have sold it on the open market. They explained that as they were praying and fasting about it, Chip's name came to mind. Did he happen to know anyone who might be interested? "Yes, they're living in our attic!" Chip exclaimed. Kevin and Laura bought the house *that night*, and they were soon hosting a male exchange student from Russia. Hearing and obeying the voice of the Lord impacted his life as well as Kevin and Laura's and the students who followed.

The more we grow in hearing God, the closer we will be drawn to him, and the greater impact we will have on the world. I want to encourage you to be open to however God may want to speak to you. Don't box him into patterns. Make it a daily anticipation to seek his voice. And as his *word dwells richly in you* (Colossians 3:16), the mark of listening will resonate on the path you leave behind.

Possibly the hardest time to hear is when we experience the resounding echoes of disappointment. Not only is it difficult to hear God in those seasons, but also the raucous clamor caused by disappointment can silence all else. God, however, leads us through our discouragements, using them to forge in us deeper grains of yet another mark—the mark of trust.

DIGGING DEEPER

1. How would you describe the importance of hearing God?
2. When has your faith specifically been strengthened by the Word of God?

3. Describe your pattern of Bible reading and prayer.

4. Which one of the hindrances in hearing God are you most susceptible to? What can help you overcome this?

5. Are there any words God has spoken to you that you need to recall?

6. How has hearing God resulted in a greater understanding of his love for you?

7. How has hearing God's directives allowed you to have a clear impact in the world?

CHAPTER 12

WHEN DISAPPOINTMENTS COME
THE MARK OF TRUST

That man is perfect in faith who can come to God in the utter dearth of his feelings and desires, without a glow or an aspiration, wandering forgetfulness, and say to Him, 'Thou art my refuge'.
—George McDonald
Unspoken Sermons

THE DAY FINALLY arrived. We had packed up our pull trailer and said our goodbyes. Our family was headed out West for a five-week vacation to visit national parks. We had been planning this trip for over two years, and it was at long last materializing. I was excited!

We spent our first night in Wauseon, Ohio. I woke up bright and early the next morning, and since the rest of the family was still asleep, I decided to slip away quietly to have my devotions. It felt chilly, and I had spotted a Burger King nearby, so I thought it would be quite romantic to take my Bible and notebook and meet God for coffee at BK.

I walked in, got my drink, found a booth, and was ready to have a wonderful little time on the first day of vacation. But it didn't go as I'd imagined. First, the *most annoying* music was playing over the sound system. Second, the coffee was *horrible*; in fact, it was the worst I had ever tasted in my life. And third, the air conditioning was running full blast. I was freezing! Now if you have any inkling toward romanticism, then you will understand what a temptation it was to feel like life was falling apart—well, not quite that dramatic, but I was definitely being pulled toward discouragement. We romantics get a picture in our minds of how things should be, and when things don't go accordingly, *disappointment* starts to set in.

But as I looked out the window and saw the sun rising over our little trailer, I made a decision to shift focus. Rather than giving in to these minor disappointments, I decided to be thankful and give praise for the *bigger* picture: We had the opportunity to be there in the first place. We were going to be making *great memories* in the next few weeks. So what was the big deal about lousy coffee and irritating music! As I look back on that day, I realize that one of the ways God marks our lives with trust is by helping us to change our perspective.

Disappointments litter the human experience. They comprise the "little foxes that spoil the vine" (Song of Solomon 2:15). We encounter small everyday disappointments— like rain forcing the cancellation of a picnic—to bigger ones—like the loss of a loved one or a broken relationship. We face disappointments with ourselves: "I thought I had already dealt with that." "Why did I have to make such a stupid remark?" We get disappointed with others: when they break their commitment, when our children don't act the way we expect them to act, when no one remembers it's our birthday, when our boss doesn't give us an anticipated raise. We get disappointed with God: "Why didn't you heal my friend?" "Why did you let our church split?" We experience disappointment with the whole human race: when injustice seems to win over justice, when immorality erodes our heroes, when what is evil is heralded as good. Disappointments are common and are triggered when things just don't work out the way we thought they would.

With every disappointment comes the death of an expectation or the snuffing out of a dream. Some disappointments can wound us so profoundly that we feel we never can trust in anything or anyone again. It is in those dark alleys of our minds where we find ourselves most vulnerable. If we're not careful, the dregs of disappointment will turn our faith into skepticism, our hope into cynicism, and our love into criticalness.

We are a generation of *disappointed* people. The high idealism of the 60s found no workable solutions to the problems exposed.

The confrontation of crass materialism, social injustices, and shallow relationships was needed; but without the radicalness of the cross, which brings lasting transformation, man-made solutions always fizzle into nothing. The skepticism, cynicism, and criticalness that emerged from dashed goals resulted in a wholesale withdrawal to self-centered lives.

So…disappointments are here to stay in this fallen world. But we need not remain stuck in them. Although we may have no control over their arrival, we can choose how we will respond to them. Because God works all things together for good to those who love him (Romans 8:28), he will use even our disappointments to achieve higher purposes. Sometimes he uses our disappointments to reveal areas in our lives that need to be purified, especially in relation to our view of him. Our overcoming will be determined by an increase in what we know and believe about God. Some disappointments are prompted by misunderstanding how God works. He often uses those situations to broaden our perspective and teach us how to wait on his timing. Finally, some of our dreams aren't his dreams, and he uses disappointment to redirect us to a better plan. But no matter what category of disappointment we face, it is the mark of trust that enables us to face our disillusionment and allow God to do his redemptive work.

Purify our Perspective

God may use disappointments to purify our vision, in order to help us acquire a clearer picture of who he is. Oswald Chambers writes, "If our hopes are being disappointed right now, it means they are being purified. We need to be tenacious, making the supreme effort to refuse to believe that our hero will be conquered. Our greatest fear is that Jesus and the things He stands for—love, justice, kindness—will not win out in the end.[47] When we meet disappointments, we will have reflected back to us whatever *our* image of God is. A clear perspective won't shield us from the sadness of disappointment, but with it our grief will not be accompanied by a sense of separation from God. However, if we view him as not loving enough or powerful enough to bring good out of the disappointment, the discouragement will actually intensify, as will our depth of isolation.

I picture disappointment like a solar eclipse. God's love and power—like the sun— loom huge, greater than anything in the sky. We represent the earth, totally dependent on the light that emanates from the sun. The disappointing situations we face correspond to the (relatively speaking) small moon. We know that when the sun, earth, and moon are aligned in just the right way, the tiny moon actually has the ability to block out the radiance of the sun, even though the sun is four hundred times bigger. In similar fashion, when we focus on our disappointments more than on the nature of God, those disappointments soon position themselves in such a way that they totally eclipse the light of God's sovereignty; and we walk in darkness.

Jeremiah serves as a good example of one who didn't allow disappointment to overshadow his knowledge of God. His circumstances enlarged, rather than erased, the mark of trust. Jeremiah, often referred to as "the weeping prophet," probably experienced more disappointment in his life than most of us will ever have to face. But because he didn't lose his grasp on the character of God, he was able to withstand the crushing circumstances he encountered. His trust in both God's sovereignty and compassion were evidenced throughout his life.

The third chapter of Lamentations records what most biblical scholars refer to as Jeremiah's cry when he was abandoned in a cistern, left to die because he had boldly declared the word of the Lord. It describes his utter isolation and rejection. The mocking and jeering by people would have been hard enough to withstand, but it's the feeling of being deserted by God that overwhelms him with disappointment. "He has filled me with bitter herbs and sated me with gall.... My splendor is gone and all that I had hoped from the Lord...my soul is downcast within me" (Lamentations 3:15, 18). Then Jeremiah makes a crucial turn. "Yet this I call to mind and therefore I have hope: Because of the Lord's great love we are not consumed, for his compassions never fail. They are new every morning; great is your faithfulness" (verses 21–23). He *remembers* God's nature, that he is a good, loving, and merciful God who does not enjoy seeing us afflicted. The knowledge of who God *really is* pulled Jeremiah out of the mire of his disappointment.

If our perception of God needs to be purified, he may, as Chambers suggests, be using our disappointments to help us see correctly. I remember one particular time when I was struggling with discouragement. Self-pity, negativity, hopelessness—they were all knocking at my door, looming like giants of defeat. Then I recalled what happened to David when he met a literal giant. You remember the story. David was sent to supply his brothers with food while they were in a battle against the Philistines. When David arrived, Goliath was ridiculing both Israel and God. All the soldiers were cowering in fear. But not David. He was infuriated and said, "Who is this uncircumcised Philistine that he should defy the armies of the living God?" (1 Samuel 17:26).

As I thought of that story, I suddenly realized that Satan had been lying to me about God. He had been insinuating that God didn't love me enough to hear my requests. But God was saying to me, "Why wouldn't I answer you? Why wouldn't I be attentive to your cry?" Encouraged by David's example, I picked up my "sling" and started hurling stones of truth at that old deceiver: "How dare you tell me that my God doesn't love me!" (*Smack*) "How dare you tell me that my God is not faithful!" (*Smack*) "How dare you try to convince me that my trust in him is misplaced!" (*Smack*) "God is the Almighty, the omnipotent, all-powerful Lord of the universe and the lover of my soul. He is the one who is able to work out all things for good to those who love him, and I *will* trust him to complete the work he began." (*Smack! Smack! Smack!*) That pretty much took care of my disappointments that day.

Broaden our Perspective

Sometimes we bring disappointment upon ourselves because we misunderstand God's timing in bringing plans to fulfillment. What we hope for hasn't happened in our time frame, so we give up and give in to disheartenment. Habakkuk exhorts us not to give up on our vision: "Though it linger, wait for it; it will certainly come and not delay" (2:3). He declares, "I will stand at my watch and station myself on the ramparts; I will look to see what he will say to me…" (2:1). Rather than succumb to disappointment when our vision isn't realized, like the prophet, we need to continue to wait and see what God says. We stand our watch and refuse to let our short-sightedness curtail the completion of God's plan and ours. How often do we needlessly experience disappointment only to learn that the answer was on the way? It may sound a bit trite, but the truth is that God is always on time. Or as one old preacher used to put it, "God inhabits all eternity, but he has a marvelous sense of timing."

One obstacle we must contend with in order to maintain our vision is the tendency to live in the "here and now." We have a hard time seeing beyond the current circumstances. Although most of us battle with this to some degree, children especially demonstrate this inclination. I'll never forget the homeschool evaluation I had with Josiah when he was nine years old. The evaluator was clearly impressed with his work. She was effusive in her praises, complementing him on reading, math, and writing skills. Finally, she asked him just what he might like to be when he grew up (thinking, I'm sure, he was going to say a brain surgeon or Supreme Court Justice). He thought a moment and then responded, "I think I'd like to be one of those people who puts whipped cream on pies." The evaluator roared with laughter because she thought he was joking (yet another indication of his brilliance). But I knew he was sincere. That week I had gotten a container of Redi-whip, and the aerosol can fascinated him. It was the most interesting profession he could imagine at that point in time. In his mind, what better future occupation could there possibly be?

Like Josiah, we sometimes can't see how much our "here and now" mindset limits what God wants to do. We will never grow through disappointment if we stay glued to the immediate. God wants to broaden our perspective to encompass ways that are higher than our ways and thoughts that are higher than ours (Isaiah 55:9).

Sometimes God's timing has to do with spiritual battles of which we are totally unaware. The Bible tells us of how Daniel prayed after receiving a vision from the Lord. Greatly disturbed, he fasted for three weeks, seeking understanding as to what it meant. Then an angel appeared to Daniel and said, "Since the first day that you set your mind to gain understanding and to humble yourself before your God, your words were heard and I have come in response to them. But the prince of the Persian kingdom resisted me twenty-one days. Then Michael, one of the chief princes, came to help me, because *I was detained …*" (Daniel 10:12–13, emphasis mine). The answer Daniel was seeking was delayed through no fault of his own. A war was raging in the spiritual realm that was affecting what was happening on the earth. Likewise, we don't know what spiritual battle may be transpiring in regards to our hopes and dreams. Some things may have to happen in the spiritual realm before things can be realized in the natural. Our job is to remain diligent in prayer.

At times we bring disappointment on ourselves, not because we are confused with God's timing, but simply because we misinterpret the events that are in front of us. I could list numerous times of where I have incorrectly "connected the dots." The result of my misperceptions was disappointment. For example, one time I was working on a project and I e-mailed a portion of it to a friend, asking for her general feedback. A few days later, I received a note back, explaining that she didn't want to critique it because of past negative experiences she'd had in assessing a friend's work. I assumed that she had looked at what I'd done and didn't like it, and this was her gracious way of not hurting my feelings. I was flooded with disappointment. But I need not have been. She honestly didn't want to get involved, so she hadn't even read it! I went through unnecessary discouragement because I had assessed the situation based on my limited knowledge and assumption, resulting in the wrong conclusion.

My cousin Carla found disappointment to both purify and broaden her perspective. She and her husband, Rick, had always desired to have a big family. They already had two daughters, and Carla was pregnant for the third time. But something went wrong, and she miscarried. When she miscarried again on her fourth pregnancy, it was discovered that she carried a defective gene which could cause severe deformities and most often, miscarriage. Even though they knew it would be risky, Carla got pregnant again. Miraculously, she carried the baby to full term, but because of the genetic abnormalities, Julia lived only two weeks. Carla was heartbroken, disappointed beyond anything she had ever before experienced.

In spite of all that had happened, Rick and Carla continued to feel a sense of incompleteness as a family. So several months after Julia's death, they began praying about adoption. They contacted an adoption agency, and upon discovering how expensive it was going to be, asked God for a clear sign as to whether or not they were to proceed. Within two weeks, they received an unexpected check for 10% of the total cost of the adoption. It gave them enough for the monetary down payment as well as the assurance that God was affirming their decision.

Those familiar with the adoption process can understand how arduous the next few months were… adoption classes, shots, physicals, extra jobs to raise money, and literally hundreds of papers and documents mailed to China. From January to August of that year they worked diligently. At that time, after the final dossier was sent to China it took four to six weeks before prospective parents were matched with a child. But right after Rick and Carla filed theirs with the Chinese consulate, China closed their doors to further adoption. To Carla, it was like another miscarriage.

Disappointment returned in full force, and by the spring of the next year, they were ready to let go of their dream completely. Then, two significant things happened. First, a pastor and his wife, Jesse and Marcie, were visiting our church, and at two separate meetings where Pastor Jesse prayed for Rick and Marcie prayed for Carla, each one gave the same word of encouragement: *Don't go back on what the Lord told you.* Second, they received a check for the exact amount of money it would take to renew all their forms. Carla said at that point she began to *choose* to trust God rather than give in to further disappointment. And hope slowly began to rise again.

One month later China reopened for adoptions. Then in October, they received a picture of the little girl who would be their new daughter. And on January first, Rick and Carla brought Anna home. It had been a two-year battle of dealing with disappointment, frustration, anger, and questioning. But the joy of having Anna overrode every discouraging moment. Through it all, not only did Rick and Carla learn to persevere in spite of circumstances over which they had no control, but also their vision and trust of God altered radically. They realized that living in a fallen world will inevitably bring disappointment, but God is able and willing to turn the disappointments into good…great good.

Redirect our Perspective

Finally, God may bring sovereign detours where we have to face the fact that what we hoped for, dreamed about, and expected will never come to pass. What we desired was not God's plan. The person we wanted to spend the rest of our life with married someone else; the physical healing we prayed for never materialized; the job we sought went to another applicant; the words "I'm pregnant" never passed our lips. The key to getting through this type of disappointment comes in realizing that God's ultimate plan is *never second best*, and that nothing matters more than being in the Father's will.

In cases like this, we follow the example of Jesus when he knelt at Gethsemane and prayed, "Not my will, but yours be done" (Mark 14:36). We know of no other time when the will of Jesus differed from the Father's. But here he asked the Father to take away the cup he was about to drink. He did not refuse and never had refused to do the Father's will. He had always obeyed. Every miracle he ever had performed was in response to what he saw the Father doing. Now, following God's will would lead him to all the horrors of the crucifixion. This wasn't a piece of theater. The reality of what he was about to face roared in front of him. So he questioned, *Is there another way?* The answer penetrated his soul. There was no second plan. It was the *only* plan. And we have life today because Jesus faithfully subjected himself to it.

The Bible says that Jesus is our high priest (Hebrews 4:14–16). Because of what he suffered, he can sympathize with what we face when all our hopes come crashing down. When we encounter situations in our lives where our will does not align with God's, Jesus is able to empower us to choose the Father's will over our own.

Such was the case for Henry Lyte, when a fatal disease struck the composer at the height of his career. When he received the news that he had only a few weeks to live, he went to his study and wrote these brave words:

> I fear no foe with Thee at hand to bless,
> Ills have no weight and tears no bitterness.
> Where is death's sting? Where grave thy victory?
> I triumph still, if Thou abide with me.

Just as he was passing from this life to the next, he exclaimed in a husky whisper, "Peace. Joy."[48] If our dreams and expectations are seemingly cut short, it is essential to see that Jesus matters more than anything else. Every other goal and desire pales in light of him.

Edith Schaeffer, in her book *Affliction*, describes the importance of having God's perspective when our dreams are cut short. One of the Schaeffers' friends in Holland suddenly discovered that he had a brain tumor and only a few days left to live. When they went to visit him, they found the dying man could only speak in raspy, broken sentences. "Before...I...everything...could...do...now...I...nothing...can...do." He was referring to the ministry God had given him to college students at the University of Amsterdam. Now he felt there was nothing left—no purpose, no meaning—just stark insignificance. At that moment, Edith Schaeffer had a startling realization: perhaps the next hours and days would be the *most* important of his whole life. She was referring to the battle in the heavenlies. This is what she said to her dying friend:

> There is no one else in all history, Mr. Van der Weiden, who has had your combination of life's experiences.... Your present combination of agonies right now is unique.... You are a person in the sight of God—and of Satan. You are really one definite individual, not just a statistic, and perhaps the next hours or days are the most important...in your life. You still have perhaps your most important work to do now, as you face the temptation to spend your remaining hours in wishing it could be otherwise or blaming God. Instead of that, you tell God you really trust him implicitly and love him in the midst of this circumstance. No one else has this particular portion of the battle to take part in, nor this particular victory to win for the Lord.[49]

She was pointing out that none of us know which is the *most important* moment of our lives. What we consider our lowest ebb may in reality be our finest hour. We don't know how many demons we're wrestling against at any given turn. Every time we come face to face with disappointment, a spiritual battle rages, and it is our opportunity to ask God to help us to trust him in spite of the circumstances and not yield to the darkness of despondency.

The Schaeffers soon had the occasion to apply this outlook in their own lives. Not long after Edith Schaeffer had written about Mr. Van der Weiden's situation, Dr. Schaeffer was diagnosed with lymphoma. While preparing for an operation at the Mayo Clinic, the Schaeffers clasped hands and prayed, "Don't let any one of us stop trusting you now, Lord. Please may our love be real for you—solid oak, not a thin veneer. This is the time that counts for your glory; don't let us blow it…Please, Father, give us victory in whatever the present battle is in the heavenlies. May Satan be disappointed."[50] …And may Satan be the one disappointed, crushed, and defeated in the battles you are facing.

We all encounter disappointments in life, but as we yield our circumstances to God, he is able to purify, broaden, or redirect the way we look at them. As we chose to be marked with trust in the One who works all things for our good, we discover a rejuvenation of faith, a renewal of hope, and a restoration of love.

Closely related to the mark of trust is the mark of hope. God wants to forge in our character the kind of hope that "does not disappoint" (Romans 5:3–5), and to do this he often takes us on a road marked with suffering.

DIGGING DEEPER

1. What are some areas of disappointment you have had to face?
2. What are some "lies" the enemy might whisper in an attempt to weaken your trust in God?
3. When has disappointment come as a result of God's timing being different from yours?
4. Can you think of times when discouragement has been the result of "misconnecting the dots"?
5. Have you experienced "sovereign detours" in your life? What has enabled you to embrace them?
6. How might the awareness of spiritual battles help us to deal with disappointment?

CHAPTER 13

FEATHER OR ANCHOR?
THE MARK OF HOPE

After all that I've been through, now I realize the truth, that I must go through the valley to stand upon the mountain of God.
—Third Day
Mountain of God

EMILY DICKINSON PENNED an interesting perspective on hope. In one of her poems, she wrote, "Hope is the thing with feathers that perches in the soul...."[51] With all due respect to Miss Dickinson, I really dislike that poem because I find it to be so accurately descriptive of my experience with hope. Hope comes like a little bird, lands on my soul, and cheers me up. Then the winds of circumstance blow, and the little bird flies away, leaving me in despair. After a while, she comes to perch again, but again flies away, perches, then flies away....

What about you? Is that the kind of hope you experience?

How different the scriptural depiction of hope is—in fact, it's almost the exact opposite of a feather. Hebrews 6:19 says, "We have this hope as an anchor for the soul, firm and secure." It's an anchor that digs deep, immovable amidst the shifting tides of people and situations. It remains firm because it enters the heavenly sanctuary and is moored to God himself.

That's the kind of hope I want to be marked with. It's the kind of hope we find depicted in Romans 5:2–5, where we see that hope comes through a process: "…And we rejoice in the hope of the glory of God. Not only so, but we also rejoice in our sufferings, because we know that suffering produces perseverance; perseverance, character; and character, hope. And hope does not disappoint us." An understanding of this progression gives us insight on how to catch that "thing with feathers." It will help us to develop the kind of hope that doesn't fly away or disappoint—the kind that has a mark as deep and fixed as an anchor.

Hope in the Glory of God

This involves getting the big picture. And there is no bigger picture than the glory of God. But what do we mean when we say the "glory of God?" *Webster's Seventh New Collegiate Dictionary* defines glory as "praise, honor or distinction; highly commendable; resplendence; magnificence; renown." It is what, according to Romans 3:23, we have all fallen short of because of our sin. Our sin took away the glory of God, making us *not praiseworthy, dishonorable, not commendable, not magnificent, and without renown.* But that glory is what God intended for us from the beginning. We lost it, but through Christ, we can find it again. Christ within is "the hope of glory" (Colossians 1:27). When we receive his redemptive work on the cross, we are restored to what we were created for in the first place. So the necessity of detaching ourselves from looking at life only in terms of the present is fundamental to developing the mark of hope.

The glory of God provides the broader perspective that reflects what is lasting and eternal as opposed to the transitory and impermanent. For no matter how desperately we hope for something in this life, once we obtain it, a new desire appears. I've met single women who lamented, "If I just had a husband, I would be content." Soon after, the object of their contentment turns to "if only I had a baby." Once that desire is met, then "maybe another baby," and then…and then…. Sometimes the desire is so short-lived that just the anticipation of what we hope for brings greater satisfaction than the actual fulfillment. Looking back, have you ever realized that you enjoyed the thought of opening a gift more than the gift itself? This reminds me of my son.

When Josiah was twelve years old, more than anything, he wanted an Xbox for Christmas. The weeks and months leading up to Christmas were saturated with incessant requests and pleas. In school, he wrote a persuasive paper on why the Xbox was better than any other game system. He constructed an advertisement for it in art. One day he actually got teary-eyed as he conveyed to his father how he didn't see any way he could ever save up enough money to buy one. We had always said "no"—too expensive, too time consuming, too addictive—but finally we decided to get it for him. Christmas morning brought screams and shouts of joy as he pulled the Xbox out of its package. It was a great surprise. But his fascination with it lasted for less than a year before it got old and he moved on to electric guitars.

Temporary desires offer short-lived satisfactions. They were never intended to do otherwise. The sufferings we experience are momentary as well. Yet they are the next step used to develop hope and its perspective of the big picture.

Suffering

Romans 8:17–18 says, "We are heirs of God and co-heirs with Christ *if* we share in his sufferings *in order* that we may also share in his glory" (emphasis mine). From this passage it becomes clear that if we want to share in the glory of God we must go through suffering. As much as I would like to tell you that pain can be bypassed on the road to hope, the truth is that there are no shortcuts.

When the human soul goes through suffering, the natural inclination is to become self-absorbed, to "close our eyes" to everything else around us and dwell on the pain. We need an outside source to pull us out of the pain so we don't drown in it. This is precisely what Scripture exhorts us to do: "Let us fix our eyes on Jesus, the author and perfecter of our faith, who for the joy set before him endured the cross…consider him… so that you will not grow weary and lose heart" (Hebrews 12:2–3). Jesus had a focal point outside of himself—the joy he knew was coming. That's what enabled him to endure. If we are to bear suffering without losing heart, we are told to make Jesus our focal point. The word "fix" means to remove our eyes from one thing and shift our gaze to another. Rather than staring at the difficulty, we are to consider him. And no other passage of Scripture helps us to do that more than Psalm 22.

Most biblical scholars agree that the anguish described in Psalm 22 reflects Jesus' passion on the cross. It begins, "My God, my God, why have you forsaken me?" Isn't that often where our suffering starts as well? *Why God? Why me? Where are you? You seem so far away. Why aren't you answering me?* It seems that God has turned his back on us. The psalmist recalls how God had delivered those who had gone before: "They cried to you and were saved; in you they trusted and were not disappointed." But rather than bringing comfort, the knowledge of how God had helped them only intensified his own despair. Have you ever experienced that? Well-meaning people telling you of how God met them served only to reinforce the conviction that he's there for everyone but you? Next, the psalmist cries, "But I am a worm and not a man..." This was not a lapse into self-pity. He was being brutally honest. He was being scorned, mocked, and despised. The fury of hell was being leashed against him: "...strong bulls of Bashan encircle me. Roaring lions tearing their prey open their mouths wide against me." We, too, must be honest about our suffering and acknowledge what we're going through. We can't put on a "happy church face" and expect relief. Fake spirituality is worthless and only increases our isolation.

In verse 19, the psalmist makes a dramatic shift. Even though he feels abandoned and rejected by both God and man, he manages to lift his head once more and cry out for deliverance. "O my Strength, come quickly to help me..." How often is it that when we least *feel* like asking again, when we think *I've done it before, why should it be any different this time*, but then somehow manage to go against our emotions, the first ray of victory dawns?

The psalmist then chooses to praise God by confessing his hope: "I will declare your name to my brothers." The fog starts to clear. No longer is he asking why he's been forsaken. "He has not hidden his face...but has listened to [my] cry for help." The vision once again comes into focus as he returns to "the theme of his praise." His suffering will result in God's ultimate purpose being accomplished. "All the ends of the earth will remember and turn to the Lord." He can endure the agony because the focal point of the joy set before him has secured his victory. Hope in the glory of God came back into focus. It is essential that we, too, lift our myopic eyes toward the larger picture. We must know with certainty that our sufferings are intended to serve a greater purpose. It is not all for naught.

Suffering Produces Perseverance

James Dobson made an astute observation: "We are in a spiritual war, with a deadly foe tracking us every hour of the day. We need to be in the best shape possible to cope with the doubts and arrows he hurls. Flabby, overindulged, pampered Christians just don't have the stamina to fight this battle. So the Lord puts us on a spiritual treadmill to keep us in good fighting position."[52] If our suffering is to produce perseverance, we have to allow ourselves to get on the treadmill. At some point in our lives, if not already, the sufferings we face will tempt us toward bitterness and dissatisfaction with God. We prepare ourselves for these moments by, in Dobson's words, getting in "good fighting position."

Whether we like it or not, life is a challenge. We are not going to understand everything God allows. But understanding is not a prerequisite for trusting him. Sometimes in that waiting time we just have to obey and do our duty. Discouragement and hopelessness tend to paralyze. Often depressed people find it hard to even get out of bed in the morning. But one of the ways we can position ourselves to let hope awaken is to get moving. There's a wonderful line in *Anne of Green Gables* when Anne is facing a difficulty. "Anne had looked at her duty courageously in the face and found it a friend—as duty ever is when we meet it frankly."[53] Duty is a friend, especially in times of discouragement because it calls us out of ourselves and forces us to act responsibly. It keeps us on the right road until we see the Lord's hand again.

In doing our duty, we learn to persevere. I think of Peter after he just had come in from fishing all night and caught nothing. No doubt he was tired, weary, discouraged, and ready to go home. But Jesus got in the boat and told him to go out deeper and try again. Scripture doesn't record any great inspirational thoughts Peter had at that moment. Simply because Jesus said so, he let the nets down. We see no passion, no hope, no faith, just *obedience* and a *willingness* to try again. What followed was a miraculous catch of fish.

Some of us tend to live *Saturday* lives, fixed somewhere between Good Friday and Resurrection Sunday. When it appears that our dilemmas have reached an impasse, discouragement seems as set as the stone on the empty tomb. But doing whatever the Lord says, even if we've tried it before, will put us on the path to that resurrected life. When the heartbroken women went to the tomb to put spices on Jesus' body, they were, in a sense, just "doing their duty." But that duty led them to the miracle of an empty grave.

One story that has encouraged me to persevere is the story of Adam Taliaferro. Adam, whose ambition since he was six years old was to play in the NFL, won a scholarship to play football at Penn State. Not only was Adam a tremendous athlete and honors student, he was also humble and gracious and well-liked by everyone. He was a rising star. In 2000, he played for Penn State as a true freshman. But his career ended abruptly when in the last minutes of the game against Ohio State, Adam received a severe spinal cord injury. The odds that he ever would walk again were three in one hundred. But Adam didn't give in to self-pity or despair. He believed he would walk again. And so did his parents, even when nothing was happening.

Some of the hospital staff thought the family was in denial. Then one night as Adam's dad was crying out to God for some kind of sign, he received a call from the hospital. Adam had slightly moved his foot. It was the first movement of any kind since the injury. Progress after that was sporadic. Doctors disagreed. Sometimes Adam would pass a pin prick test and sometimes he wouldn't. But the Taliaferros continued to hold on to their hope. Finally, Adam's progress picked up, and through the intensity of physical therapy, he began showing improvement not just month-to-month, but week-to-week and day-to-day.

On September 1, 2001, less than a year after his injury, and contrary to all the doctors' predictions, Adam led his PSU team onto the football field before a sellout crowd of 109,313 people, who all stood to their feet to honor him. Coach Joe Paterno said, "Adam Taliaferro's story is…the most gallant, uplifting and inspiring one I can imagine…. Adam will never play football again. But he has had an impact on everyone associated with the game, an impact that transcends any accomplishments he might have achieved as an athlete. Adam is our miracle. From this day forward every time we see him or hear of him, we will contemplate the power of prayer, of a positive approach to adversity, of dogged determination, and of unconditional love."[54]

When I first read Adam's story, tears ran down my face—right in the middle of Borders Bookstore—because I was going through things in my life that made me just want to "turn in my uniform." But I knew God had led me to the book about Adam's life, and it was as if he was saying, "How dare you think about hanging up your uniform!" I thought about how Adam's parents stubbornly refused to give up. I thought of all the rigors of physical therapy Adam endured and of how he tried and tried again and again just to be able to walk. Suddenly, my pain was put in a different perspective. My circumstances didn't miraculously change, but I discovered a new determination to persevere.

Have you ever felt like you wanted to hang up your uniform, that you just couldn't do it anymore? Do you feel that way now? Don't quit. Let God teach you how to persevere through your suffering. It will prepare you for the next step.

Perseverance Produces Character

I've come to believe that the progression from perseverance to character is the area where most Christians stumble. No matter where we are in our walk with God, he always seems to be working on our character. It's not that he doesn't love us just the way we are, but it's because of that love that he's not content to have us stay riddled with flaws and weaknesses. He wants to push us up a notch from wherever we might be. So he allows situations to enter our lives to make us nobler, more compassionate, and more courageous than we've ever been before. And suffering is often the means used to get us there.

One of the best books I've ever read on this subject is *Making Sense Out of Suffering* by Boston College Professor Peter Kreeft. In this book, he shows how hope in the midst of suffering comes only as we are able to look past the veneer of the surface issues and embrace what is causing the deeper, richer grains in the wood. He has a wonderful way of outlining clues God has given us from philosophers, artists, and prophets that point to the meaning found in our struggles.[55]

For example, Kreeft explains how suffering is shown to be purposed for something higher even in children's stories. His observations took me back to a poster I had plastered on my wall when I was in graduate school. It was from the classic *Velveteen Rabbit*, and it recounted the conversation between the Skin Horse and the Rabbit, where the Skin Horse explains how pain plays a major part in the process of becoming real. The Horse says, "That's why it doesn't often happen to people who break easily, or have sharp edges, or who have to be carefully kept. Generally, by the time you are Real, most of your hair has been loved off, and your eyes drop out and you get loose in the joints and very shabby. But these things don't matter at all, because once you are Real you can't be ugly, except to people who don't understand."[56]

Everyone desires to live a meaningful story. Who wants to look back on their life and say, "*Bor-ing!*"? Yet it's often the troubles we encounter and survive that make our lives remarkable. For most of us, when the part of our story turns to affliction, we don't care about meaning, we just want out. If, however, we knew that in the end going through the difficulties would make our lives more significant, more virtuous, more *interesting*, I'm convinced we would choose to go through them. That reminds me of our family vacations. If anything, they accurately could be called *interesting*.

Most families have vacations to relax and refresh. Not the Toews! Even if that was our original intent, we are infamous for family vacations that illustrate the principle of perseverance developing character. We have hanging on the wall of our pull trailer a list of all our vacations: when, where, who may have joined us, and next to all that, the disaster we experienced. I'm not kidding. We've suffered everything from sun poisoning to midnight gale winds forcing us to take down our tents, to bicycles flying off the back of the trailer and smashing the windshield of the car behind us. During our last vacation, we didn't even camp and still experienced a crisis. Chip, Bethany, and I were taking a little hike around our motel, and I fell and severely sprained my ankle. It was so bad that I had to be carted around Williamsburg in a wheelchair. This actually wasn't that bad for me, but by the end of the day, the rest of the family was exhausted from having to push me!

Many of our disasters have involved our vehicles. It seems something always goes wrong with our car. Twice we borrowed my father-in-law's jeep, and twice it broke down. Once we even borrowed our *mechanic's* car, and the ignition box died while we were in line on the ferry to Ocracoke at the Outer Banks in North Carolina. But the all-time character-building disaster occurred the year we went to Disney World when Bethany was five. We had spent the whole day there, not leaving until the park closed. Close to midnight, we piled into our Cherokee, completely worn out and ready for bed. But on the way back to our campground, smoke started pouring out from the front of the jeep. Chip pulled over, lifted the hood, and the whole engine burst into flames! There was no way the problem was going to be remedied at that time of night, so we had to take a cab back to our campground. Who takes a $40 cab ride at two in the morning to a campsite? The Toews on vacation! The next day we found out that the car was irreparable. Fortunately, our friends Brad and Marianne Wills were in Florida for a reunion. They were driving back to Massachusetts, and they offered us a ride home. So, towing a U-Haul filled with our camping gear, the five of us packed into their little Honda for a nineteen-hour trek back to Pennsylvania.

As troublesome as those vacations were, I wouldn't trade them for all the beach houses in New Jersey. Although we weren't laughing at the time, we look back now and actually are *thankful*—not only for the unique memories, but also for the way we grew through them. And they definitely would never be characterized as *bor-ing*!

Character Produces Hope that Doesn't Disappoint

Hope that doesn't disappoint, that doesn't fly away when troubles come, is a hope that has been developed through suffering, perseverance, and tried character. It's a process that binds us to the Lord. Isaiah 40:30 says that those "who hope in the Lord will renew their strength." The Hebrew word for hope is *qawah*. It means to bind together by twisting. The implication is that we have drawn so close to God through the suffering that it's as if we are entwined with him. No wonder, then, that our strength is renewed. How could we remain weak when bound so tightly to the strongest power in the universe?

Hope that doesn't disappoint is also hope that finds its strength in the Word of God. Romans 15:4 says, "For everything that was written in the past was written to teach us, so through endurance and the encouragement of the Scriptures we might have hope." As we look to Scripture, we find there is no hopeless situation that we might face that the Word of God does not address.

What about financial difficulties, when our very livelihood is threatened? Habakuk 3:16–18 says, "I will wait patiently…. Though the fig tree does not bud and there are no grapes on the vines, though the olive crop fails and the fields produce no food, though there are no sheep in the pen and no cattle in the stalls, *yet* I will rejoice in the Lord" (emphasis mine). Israel is being invaded, but Habakuk's response is not despair. He says he will wait patiently for things to turn around. No matter what happens, he is determined to wait on the Lord. It's as if he lists every possible catastrophe that could be encountered while he is waiting: No crops…he will wait. No food…he'll wait. No cattle…he'll wait. No sheep…he'll wait. The footnote in my Bible says this is one of the strongest affirmations of faith in all of Scripture. And it is written to give us hope so that: When we don't have money for this month's bills, we can wait. When we lose a job, we can wait. Even if the stock market crashes, we can wait and not lose hope.

But what about relational breakdowns? Sometimes those can be more devastating than financial troubles. Micah 7:5–7 says, "Now is the time of their confusion. Do not trust a neighbor, put no confidence in a friend. Even with her who lies in your embrace be careful of your words. For a son dishonors his father and a daughter rises up against her mother, a daughter-in-law against her mother-in-law; a man's enemies are the members of his own household." How devastating! Husbands and wives not trusting each other, children rebelling, separation and disintegration of friendships—it sounds a lot like our society today, doesn't it? Yet look what Micah says in the midst of this destruction: "But as for me, I watch in hope for the Lord, I wait for God my Savior; my God will hear me." This is written to give us hope.

Even for situations that are impossible to resolve by human standards, we find encouragement in Scripture. Daniel 2 relays the situation where king Nebuchadnezzar demanded that someone in his kingdom not only interpret his dream, but also tell him what the dream was in the first place. If no one could do this *impossible* task, all the wise men in the land would be executed. Daniel, as one of the king's wise men, sought the Lord, and the Lord revealed the dream to him. When Daniel went before the king, he said, "No wise man, enchanter, magician or diviner can explain to the king the mystery he has asked about, *but there is a God in heaven* who reveals mysteries" (emphasis mine). *But there is a God in heaven*... Are there "impossible situations" in your life right now? If so, I would encourage you to do what I did after I read this passage. I listed each circumstance and then wrote beside every one: *but there is a God in heaven.* What a great way to finish a sentence! Whatever circumstance we face, because *there is a God in heaven*, we have reason to hope.

How about you? What are your sorrows? What situation in your life seems like it could never work out for good? What hurt is so deep that you think it can't be healed? What disappointment is so great that you assume it can't be redeemed? What sin has marred you so badly that you believe the shame can never be erased? Have you been betrayed or rejected? Have you failed? *There is a God in heaven,* and there is *nothing* that has come your way that God does not intend to use for good; otherwise he would never have let it come.

Psalm 130:5 says, "I wait for the LORD, my soul waits, and in his word I put my hope." When translated, the word "hope" in this verse means "anxious expectation." God wants us to be anxiously awaiting him. We are to be like watchmen on the wall who are waiting for morning. They have no doubt morning will come, but they must wait in the dark. And so must we at times.

God calls us to moor our anchor to him and make known to others the mark of hope—a mark of hope that carries us through the difficulties in life. A mark of hope that enables us to reach noble heights. A mark of hope that doesn't end here...a mark that leads us to eternity...

Digging Deeper

1. Would you characterize your hope as more like a feather or an anchor? Why?
2. What was something you longed for that after obtaining it didn't bring the fulfillment you thought it would?
3. How has a "joy set before" you helped you to endure a time of suffering?
4. Have you experienced a time when you felt like God had forsaken you? What helped you come through?
5. While going through difficulties, has there been a time when "duty has been your friend"?
6. Have you ever felt like "hanging up your uniform"?
7. How has the need to persevere caused your character to be refined?
8. How has the Word of God strengthened you in helping you to wait on the Lord?
9. What seemingly "impossible situation" are you facing right now in which you need to declare, "…but there's a God in heaven"?

CHAPTER 14

HEAVEN...THERE'S NO PLACE LIKE HOME

THE MARK OF ETERNITY

Our Father refreshes us on the journey with some pleasant inns, but will not encourage us to mistake them for home.
—C. S. Lewis
The Problem of Pain

EVERY CHRISTMAS OUR family, like many others in the church, orders poinsettias to help decorate the sanctuary for the season. After the Christmas Eve service, everyone takes their poinsettias home. One particular year, since we were going to visit my mom in Ohio the next day, we decided to take a poinsettia to her. We packed it up in the car with all the rest of our bags, suitcases and gifts and gave it to her when we arrived. She put it on a table in the living room and watered it regularly. A few weeks later, after we were back home, I was talking with her on the phone and she told me how surprised she had been at how nice the poinsettia had stayed (she attributed that to putting ice cubes in it instead of actual water). But eventually, when *none* of the leaves fell off, her curiosity was aroused. A closer inspection revealed that the poinsettia she had been watering all those weeks was artificial. I had picked up the wrong one! The point: When we center only on temporal things and not the eternal, it's like watering artificial plants. It's not *really* the real thing.

Although the Bible tells us that God has made everything beautiful in its time, he has also "set eternity in the hearts of men" (Ecclesiastes 3:11). That mark of eternity whispers to us that we are made for something other than this world. And actually, the greater our understanding of eternity, the better we are able to define the significance of what we do here. Many have observed that it's those with the clearest view of heaven that make the biggest difference on the earth. But it seems for most of us that eternity, or heaven, remains a vague notion. We recognize a restlessness in ourselves, yet it seems we try to quiet it by becoming even more, not less, focused on things that will eventually pass away. My guess is that few of us give much consideration to eternity at all.

Why don't we think about heaven more? If we did, what difference would it make? And if we were to think about it, what would comprise our thoughts? I began to ask myself such questions, and the answers I discovered made me more aware of this *mark of eternity* set in my heart… and a bit homesick for my eternal home.

Why don't we think about heaven more?

When I first started studying about heaven, I thought it would be interesting to look it up on the internet. The thought did cross my mind that if someone asked me what I was doing right then and I responded that I was looking for heaven online, that it would sound pretty bizarre, nevertheless… Did you know that there are 19,100, 000 references to heaven on Google? Some of the references listed included the following:

- Dog heaven
- Hubcap heaven
- Television heaven
- Stationery heaven
- Pin ball heaven
- Home brew heaven
- Nerds heaven (I'll let your imagination run with that one)

Obviously, the term "heaven" has come to mean a lot of different things in our society, and as a result, the meaning of the real heaven has gotten blurred. I believe this contributes not only to our lack of thinking about it, but also to our lack of longing for it.

When many people think of heaven, they have medieval images of jewels, harps, puffy clouds, and cherub angels. Some people tend to think of heaven as this changeless, static state of perfection. I've heard people say things like, "There's going to be unending praise and worship in heaven, so if you don't like it here, you're in for a hard time there." Well, I love to praise and worship, but it's hard for me to imagine *doing nothing but singing praises to God forever.* Scripture says that "no eye has seen, no ear has heard, no mind has conceived what God has prepared for those who love him" (1 Corinthians 2:9). Yet, as the symbolism of heaven gets filtered through our contemporary minds, we end up with wooden images of what heaven is like, and if we were honest, some of us might admit that it all seems a bit dull. We don't hope for heaven or think about it because the images we have elicit neither our interest nor our love. That is Satan's victory. I suggest we have the wrong images.

A second reason we don't think about or long for heaven is a result of a lack of instruction. We're actually not trained very well in how to think about life twenty years from now, far less in eternity. We are a society obsessed with the present. It's as if today is all that exists. And the church is not immune. On the extreme right, Christianity stands as the present means to greater personal prosperity; on the left, a social gospel seeks primarily to liberate the poor. I'm not suggesting that these aren't valid issues to discuss, but when the focus remains on *this world,* our perspective becomes flawed. Most of us probably don't fall in either of these extremes; nonetheless, it is hard not to think primarily in terms of the present. All too often we aspire to no more than being comfortable.

In his lectures, Francis Schaeffer often warned about falling into the trap of "personal peace and affluence"—as long as my life runs smoothly, that's all that really matters. I recall one sermon where he presented a powerful illustration of the "old man who continued trimming his hedge." The whole world was falling apart, but "the old man continued trimming his hedge." People all around were headed toward eternity in hell, but "the old man continued trimming his hedge." His mindset extended no further than his front yard. Like the old man, we, too, can become consumed only with this life. God wants us to think BIG—so big that we're not constrained to the earth at all. As Lewis put it, "If we aim for heaven, we'll get earth thrown in, but if we aim for the earth, we'll get neither." [57]

Many of the saints have written about yet another reason why we don't think about heaven. We don't recognize that it is heaven we're really longing for. The argument is made that every natural desire we have points to a corresponding object that can satisfy that desire. We satisfy our hunger with food, our fatigue with rest, our loneliness with relationships. But there remains in every person a desire which nothing on earth can meet. That desire can only be met by something outside the earth, and that something is heaven. Let's look at some quotes from people who had this perspective:

- Augustine wrote, "Thou hast made us for thyself. Our hearts are restless until they rest in Thee." [58]
- Deitrich Bonhoeffer, when being led to his execution, whispered to his fellow prisoners, "For me it is the beginning." [59]
- William Wilberforce said, "Christianity proposes not to extinguish our natural desires. It promises to bring the desires under just control and direct them to their true object." [60]
- Missionary Jim Elliot held this same view. He said, "It's not a matter of no gratification, but delayed gratification in the pursuit of ultimate gratification…. He is no fool who gives what he cannot keep to gain what he cannot lose." [61]
- Author Peter Kreeft describes heaven as "the heart's deepest longing." [62]

What difference does it make?

Even if we begin to realize that we're not thinking about heaven accurately or extensively, we encounter the second question: does it really matter? I've come to the conclusion that it makes all the difference in the world, in this life as well as in the next. One author quipped that

Christians who never think about heaven are said to have the three cardinal virtues of faith, *cope,* and love, because they are Christians only for what it does for them in this life.

When we took our trip out West to visit National Parks, we had an allotted amount of time. Right before we left, we found out that Wal-Mart allows travel trailers to stay overnight free of charge in their parking lots. This was great for us, because we had to stop many times just for the night and then get back on the road the next morning to get to the parks. Obviously, at Wal-Mart there's no electrical or water hookups, no cozy campfires, no great outdoor scenery (although I always insisted we hunt for a tree to park beside). These things didn't matter. We were content because we knew we weren't at our final destination. It was just an overnighter. We could put up with the inconveniences because we knew we were going to a better place. I couldn't help but think of the parallel to our lives here on the earth. It would be a sad commentary if we were satisfied to camp at Wal-Mart when we had the opportunity to visit the Grand Canyon, Yellowstone, and Yosemite.

In a very real sense, the Bible says we should view ourselves as campers or travelers, headed for a much better place. Pity us if we hope for this life only! Both 1 Peter 2:11 and Hebrews 11:13 say that we are to live as aliens and strangers in the world; Philippians 3:20 states that our citizenship is in heaven; 2 Corinthians 5:20 declares, "...we are therefore Christ's ambassadors...." Wouldn't it be strange for us to send ambassadors to other countries, only to have them decide that they liked those countries more than their own? They would cease to be a true representative of their native land.

The application becomes clearer when we remember God's call to Abraham. "The Lord said to Abraham, 'Leave your country, your people and your father's household and go to the land I will show you. I will make you into a great nation and I will bless you'" (Genesis 12:1–2). Similarly, God is telling us to go to a place we have never seen. And he says in order to prepare, we have to leave our country, in essence, everything that is familiar to us—our language, our "culture," our goals—all our attachments. But if we do, he has promised more, more, more than we could ever receive in this land. As the father of our faith, Abraham paved the way for us to follow. "By faith, Abraham, when called to go to a place he would later receive as his inheritance, obeyed and went, even though he did not know where he was going. By faith he made his home in the Promised Land like a stranger in a foreign country; he lived in tents…. For he was looking forward to the city with foundations, whose architect and builder is God" (Hebrews 11:8–10).

Rick Warren, in *Purpose Driven Life,* describes our life on earth as a "test," a "trust," and a "temporary assignment." Everything we go through here prepares us for what lies ahead. When we see *all* of life as a test, we realize nothing we go through is insignificant. Viewing life as a trust helps us to understand the importance of doing the best we can with what we've got. Becoming aware that life is just a temporary assignment aids us in not setting contentment as our ultimate goal.[63] In contrast, today's typical mindset seems to be best reflected in the beer commercial that proclaims, "It doesn't get any better than this." This is a sad commentary.

Living in the light of eternity colors the way we see everything here, the struggles as well as the blessings. But it also affects what happens in the next life. Throughout Scripture we are told that at the end of this life we are going to be judged, first as to whether or not we received Christ as Savior, and second, for the works we have done—the one for what we believe, the other for what we do. "For we must all appear before the judgment seat of Christ, that each one may receive what is due him, for the things done while in the body, whether good or bad" (2 Corinthians 5:10). The result of this judgment will be either the gain or loss of eternal rewards.

Some may feel that the thought of rewards in heaven sounds a bit self-serving. But it all depends on our motivation. C. S. Lewis explains, "We must not be troubled by unbelievers when they say that this promise of reward makes the Christian life a mercenary affair. There are different kinds of rewards. There is the reward which has no natural connection with the things you do to earn it and is quite foreign to the desires that ought to accompany those things. Money is not the natural reward of love; that is why we call a man mercenary if he marries a woman for the sake of her money. But marriage is the proper reward for a real lover, and he is not mercenary for desiring it…. The proper rewards are not simply tacked on to the activity for which they are given, but are the activity itself in consummation."[64] The Christian who receives the rewards of heaven doesn't look upon the rewards as some kind of payoff for doing the right thing, like a celestial carrot waved in front of his or her nose. Rather, the rewards are the natural (or supernatural) by-product of the Christian's life on earth. God evidently wanted us to be aware of the rewards awaiting us or he wouldn't have enumerated so many in Scripture. I counted over twenty-five references to rewards in the New Testament. Here is a sampling of what they are and why they are given:

- God will reward those who serve him faithfully. "The time has come for judging the dead, and for rewarding your servants, the prophets, and the saints and those who reverence you name, both small and great..." (Revelation 11:18).
- He will reward every person for how he or she has lived his or her life. "For the Son of Man is going to come in his Father's glory with his angels, and then he will reward each person according to what he has done" (Matthew 16:27).
- God will reward us for how we treat the undeserving. "But love your enemies, do good to them, and lend to them without expecting to get anything back. Then your reward will be great, and you will be sons of the Most High..." (Luke 6:35).
- God rewards us for everyday acts of kindness. "I tell you the truth, anyone who gives you a cup of water in my name because you belong to Christ will certainly not lose his reward" (Mark 9:41).
- A number of passages point to rewards and blessings for those who are persecuted for Christ's sake. "Do not repay evil with evil, but with blessing, because to this you were called so that you may inherit a blessing" (1 Peter 3:9). "Blessed are you when men hate you, when they exclude and insult you and reject your name as evil, because of the Son of Man. Rejoice in that day and leap for joy, because great is your reward in heaven" (Luke 6:22–24).
- God rewards us for identifying with those who are suffering and enduring material loss. "You sympathized with those in prison and joyfully accepted the confiscation of your property because

you knew that you yourselves had better and lasting possessions. So do not throw away your confidence; it will be richly rewarded" (Hebrews 10:34–35).

- God is going to judge our works. Scripture clarifies that not all works will pass the test. "If any man builds on this foundation using gold, silver, costly stones, wood, hay or straw, his work will be shown for what it is, because the day will bring it to light. It will be revealed with fire, and the fire will test the quality of each man's work." (1 Corinthians 3:12–13). Those works that are not motivated by obedience or love will be consumed. Scripture says that even if we die a martyr's death, if it's not done from the motivation of love, *it profits us nothing* (1 Corinthians 13:3). We want to make sure our works originate from the right motivations.

Beyond a doubt, everything we do on earth will have an effect in heaven. The Lord *wants* to reward us generously. He doesn't want us to stand before him on judgment day with empty hands or hay and stubble. Nor do we want to stand before him and the only thing we have to report is, "Look, Lord, see how well I trimmed my hedge."

How then should we think about heaven?

Perhaps with the same curiosity of the child who asks, "What's heaven like?" we come to the third question. Ravi Zacharias wrote in *Recapture the Wonder,* "We talk of heaven as a place, and it is that. We talk of heaven as a feeling, and it is that. We talk of heaven as a destiny, and it is that. But it is more.... Heaven is that reality where your existence is lived to its fullest essence and the God who fashioned you leads you to the ultimate expression for which he made you."[65]

In some ways, it is easier to define what heaven is not, than what it is. Scripture tells us that in heaven there is no death, no pain, no sadness, no sin, no defeat. There will be no separation from others. No longer will we experience loneliness and isolation. No more confusion and misunderstanding. No war. No poverty. No more marks of the fall–rejection, fear, shame and guilt, and blame shifting. But heaven is far more than the absence of negatives....

Heaven is a place of complete transformation in every area of life

Jesus makes all things new. First, we will have renewed bodies. I must admit, the older I get, the more appealing this aspect of heaven becomes. Right now I'm contemplating how nice it will be to sit at a computer for an extended period of time and not get a backache! Although we don't know exactly what our new bodies may be like, we do know that they will be similar to the body Christ had after his resurrection. "Jesus...will transform our lowly bodies so that they will be like his glorious body" (Philippians 3:21). Jesus' resurrected body was not some kind of ghostly specter. He was flesh and blood. He ate and drank, walked and talked. But he could also go through walls and move in a spiritual dimension, as he was no longer bound by natural limitations.

Second, we will have transformed natures. "...and what we will be has not yet been made known. But we know that when he appears, we shall be like him for we shall see him as he is" (1 John 3:2). When we see him face to face we are changed. All the impurities of sin that have diluted who we were intended to be are washed away. Our jealousies, insecurities, and addictions cease to exist. No matter how badly we have been scarred in this life, every ugly stain will turn into a mark of beauty. In Luke 12:3 it says that there is nothing concealed that will not be disclosed, or hidden that will not be made known. But with the exposure of each sin, each careless word, each unworthy thought, our embarrassment and shame will be absorbed in Jesus' proclamation of pardon. We will be transformed in the light of his absolute goodness and forgiveness. We will comprehend for the first time just how much he has loved us, for the full extent of his grace will be displayed. I can't help but think that such an overwhelming awareness will elicit from the depths of our souls pure, eternal worship. What began on the earth when we accepted Christ as Savior will be completed in our resurrection.

Heaven is a place teeming with action

Besides being a place of complete transformation, heaven will also be a place of dynamic activity. Nothing in Scripture suggests that we are headed for a celestial retirement village in the sky where we sit in golden rocking chairs and play harps all day. There is going to be work to do, but work that has not been affected by the fall. To begin with, we will be ruling: "They will be priests of God and of Christ and will reign with Him for a thousand years" (Revelation 20:6). We will be judging: "Do you not know that we will judge angels?" (1 Corinthians 6:3). If we are ruling and judging, that means we'll be learning and communicating. All those barriers that currently keep us from understanding and being understood will be removed. That irresistible human drive to want to share with others what we've discovered will reach fulfillment. We will continually be exploring inexhaustible sources of wisdom, love, and grace (Ephesians 2:7). Far from being in some static state of changelessness, we are going to be working, judging, ruling, learning, communicating, and worshiping, but without the restraints we now experience because of the curse.

Heaven is the place of our new address

Finally, heaven is a place of ultimate security. Heaven is home. "In my Father's house are many rooms; if it were not so, I would have told you. I am going there to prepare a place for you…" (John 14:2–3). This is perhaps for me the most tangible aspect of heaven because of the compelling connotation of home.

Many years ago I left the home where I grew up in Southern Ohio, but to this day there is no place where I have felt more relaxed, more accepted, or more secure than my mom's house. And I've tried to pass that sense of security on to my children. After Bethany left for college, each time she came home I did everything I could to welcome her back. I made cheese steaks (her favorite), and in the winter I would make sure there was a fire in the fireplace. I baked cookies and cleaned her room (although I have a feeling that went unnoticed). And the first time she came home after being away, we put up big "welcome home" signs all over the house. Josiah's homecomings from college have been no less anticipated. We all—even his dog, Beau— let him know how much he's been missed.

But no matter how safe and secure we may feel in our earthly homes, it's just a taste of the home the Lord is preparing for us. Our earthly homes shape our individual identities, but in heaven, we will find the completion of our true identity. Revelation 2:17 says that we will each receive a white stone with a *new name* written on it known only to us. It will be the expression of who we really are. Far from being a place where individuals melt into some pantheistic *oneness*, in heaven I'll be more Becky Toews than I've ever been, and you will be more you. No longer will we be misunderstood or mischaracterized, because at long last we'll be known as we really are.

Sometimes I imagine reaching heaven as being similar to what happens at the end of kids' athletic events. You know how they walk through a lineup and high five each other as they shout "good game"? I picture us going through a double line, each side filled with loved ones who have gone on before. Hands raised to greet ours, they're cheering, rejoicing that we've made it home. I see Grandpa, Grandma, Aunt Noreen, Mae, Don, Joyce...all celebrating my victory. Imagine for a moment those who are waiting to welcome you. Will there be a spouse, a parent, a child, a dear friend? The terrible severing that took place on the earth will be restored in an instant, heralding a restoration that will last for eternity. And as we make it to the end of the line, nothing we've experienced on earth will compare to that moment. There, waiting to embrace us, will be the One who is the source of what we've been looking for all our lives.

A few years ago our family visited the Stonewall Jackson Memorial, the site where Jackson died in the middle of the Civil War. As usual, we took in the Ranger Program. The ranger explained how Jackson had been wounded in friendly fire by his own men. As the soldiers were moving him back to the house, they unfortunately dropped him, and he landed right on the side where he had been shot. At first, he progressed well, but pneumonia set in, and the remedy they gave him actually worsened his condition. They sent for his wife and newborn baby, hoping their presence might have a positive effect on him, but he continued to deteriorate. The last few days of his life found Jackson moving in and out of delirium. They heard him shouting orders to his men, as if he were reliving every battle he had ever fought. Then, all the delirium stopped. A great peace came over him, and he whispered, "Let us cross over the river and rest under the shade of the trees."

Just as the ranger got to this point, Bethany, who was standing across from me and next to Chip, suddenly crumbled to the floor. Her eyes rolled to the back of her head, and she fell as Chip tried to catch her. She was out. We were trying to revive her, but I can say I've never been so scared in my life. Here we were, hundreds of miles from home, and at the exact same time we were hearing of Jackson's death, my dear daughter lay unconscious on the floor. It only lasted a minute, but it seemed like an eternity before she came to and mumbled, "What happened?" She was back to her old self.

If the circumstances surrounding Jackson's death had impressed me before, Bethany's happenstance made them indelible. I have thought much about the vision of heaven Jackson obviously had before he died. All the battles he had fought in life had come to an end. He saw the shade of the trees, and he was going home to rest.

Like Stonewall Jackson, there will come a time when our battles will cease. Our sufferings will end. Our hopes will be realized. Someday we too will be beckoned to cross over the river. The mark of eternity will have taken us home.

DIGGING DEEPER

1. Examine your thoughts about heaven. Can you identify any "wrong images"?
2. How much does the aspiration of "personal peace and affluence" trap you into thinking in terms of this world only?
3. Have you experienced a restlessness or longing for something you know can't be satisfied on earth? Explain.
4. How does seeing life as a "test, a trust, and a temporary assignment" help to better prepare you for eternity?
5. Does the thought of being rewarded in heaven for what you do on earth affect you? How?
6. What is one aspect of heaven that you most anticipate?
7. Describe in your words how heaven "is the beginning" for you.

ENDNOTES

Chapter 1

1. Christina Hoff Sommers, "Teaching the Virtues." *AFA Journal* (January, 1992).
2. George Barna and Mark Hatch, *Boiling Point* (Ventura, California: Regal Books, 2001), 188-192.

Chapter 2

3. David McCullough, *1776* (New York: Simon and Shuster, 2005), 293-294.
4. Stephen Hill, *Daily Awakenings* (Ventura, California: Regal Books, 1999), November 27.
5. Ellen Vaughn, *Radical Gratitude.* (Grand Rapids, Michigan: Zondervan, 2005), 43.

Chapter 3

6. Ed Silvoso, *That None Should Perish.* (Ventura, California: Regal Books, 1994), 186.
7. Aleksandr Solzhenitsyn, Lecture at Harvard University, 1978.
8. Dorothy Sayers, *Christian Letters to a Post-Christian World.* (Grand Rapids, Michigan: Eerdmans, 1969).

9. Blaise Pascal, *Pensees* (London: Penguin Books Ltd, 1995).

Chapter 4

10. Bill Bennett, Lecture #447, Heritage Foundation, "Getting Used to Decadence: The Spirit of Democracy in Modern American," December 25, 1993.
11. Francis Schaeffer, *The Great Evangelical Disaster* (Westchester, Illinois: Crossway Books, 1984).
12. Francis Schaeffer, *True Spirituality* (Wheaton, Illinois: Tyndale House Publishers, 1982), 25-30.
13. David Stick, *Graveyard of the Atlantic* (Chapel Hill: University of North Carolina Press, 1952), 166-168.
14. Martin Luther King, Jr. Speech in Detroit, Michigan, June 23, 1963.

Chapter 5

15. C. S. Lewis, *Mere Christianity* (New York: Macmillian Publishing Company, 1960), 161.
16. Brennan Manning, *Ruthless Trust* (San Francisco: HarperCollins Publishers, 2000), 32-33.
17. David Wells, *Losing Our Virtue* (Grand Rapids, Michigan: William B. Eardmans Publishing Company, 1999), 4.
18. Martin Seligman, *Learned Optimism* (New York: Simon and Shuster, 1990), Chapter 2.
19. Brennan Manning, *Ruthless Trust* (San Francisco: HarperCollins Publishers, 2000), 117.
20. Quoted in John Ortberg, *If You Want To Walk on Water You've Got to Get Out of the Boat* (Grand Rapids, Michigan: Zondervan, 2001), 88.
21. Author unknown. *Be Thou My Vision.*

Chapter 6

22. Brennan Manning, *Reflections for Ragamuffins* (New York: HarperCollins Publishers, 1998), x.

23. John Woodbridge, gen. ed., *More Than Conquerors* (Chicago: The Moody Bible Institute, 1992), 26-31.

24. J. Sidlow Baxter, *Explore the Book* (Grand Rapids: Zondervan Publishing House, 1966), 172.

25. Mike Bickle, *Song of Songs* (Kansas City: Grace Training Center of Kansas City, 1995).

26. C. S. Lewis, *The Horse and His Boy* (New York: Macmillian Publishing Co. Inc., 1954), 158.

Chapter 7

27. William Shakespeare, *The Merchant of Venice*, Act 4, Scene 1.

28. Corrie ten Boom, *Tramp for the Lord* (Fort Washington, Pennsylvaina: Christian Literature Crusade and Fleming H. Revell Company, 1974), 55-57.

29. Roy Hession, *The Calvary Road* (Fort Washington, Pennsylvania: Christian Literature Crusade, 1950).

30. C. S. Lewis, *Mere Christianity* (New York: Macmillian Publishing Company, 1960), 104.

31. Timothy Keller, *The Prodigal God* (New York: Dutton, 2008), 83.

Chapter 8

32. Oswald Chambers, *My Utmost for His Highest* (USA: Dodd, Mead & Company, Inc., 1935), 353.

33. John Foxe, *Foxe's Book of Martyrs* (New Kinsington, PA: Whitaker House, 1981), 340.

34. Andrew Murray, *Absolute Surrender* (Chicago: Moody Press, 1895), Chapter V

35. Donald Miller, *Blue Like Jazz* (Nashville: Thomas Nelson Publishers, 2003), 218.

36. Dietrich Bonhoeffer, *The Cost of Discipleship* (New York: Simon and Schuster, 1950),47.

37. Michael Card, *A Violent Grace* (Sisters, Oregon: Multinomah Publishers, Inc., 2000).

Chapter 9

38. Cleavant Derricks, *Just a Little Talk with Jesus*

Chapter 10

39. James Dobson, *Parenting Isn't for Cowards* (Illinois: Tyndale House Publishers, Inc., 1987).
40. Dan Allender, *Sabbath* (Nashville: Thomas Nelson, 2009), 142.
41. Tony Snow, "Cancer's Unexpected Blessings," *Christianity Today*, Vol. 57, No. 7, July, 2007.
42. Winston Churchill's first speech as the new British Prime Minister to the House of Commons, May 13, 1940.
43. Y. Shoda, W. Mischel, & P. K. Peake, "Predicting adolescent cognitive and self regulatory competencies from preschool delay of gratification," *Developmental Psychology*, 1990, 26 (6), 978–986.
44. Frederick Loomis, "The Tiny Foot," *Christmas by the Hearth,* Rick Blanchette, ed., (Wheaton, Illinois: Tyndale House Publishers, Inc., 1996), 151-159.

Chapter 11

45. C. S. Lewis, *The Silver Chair* (New York: Macmillan Publishing Co., Inc. 1953), 21.
46. Fanny Crosby, *Draw Me Nearer*. Public Domain.

Chapter 12

47. Oswald Chambers, *My Utmost for His Highest* (New York: Dodd, Mead and Company, 1963), 53.
48. Robert J. Morgan, *Then Sings My Soul* (Nashville: Thomas Nelson Publishers, 2003), 119.
49. Edith Schaeffer, *Affliction* (Old Tappan, New Jersey: Fleming H. Revell Company, 1978), 67–75.
50. Edith Schaeffer, *The Tapestry* (Waco Texas: Word Books, 1981), 615.

Chapter 13

51. Emily Dickinson, *The Complete Poems of Emily Dickinson*. (Boston: Little, Brown, 1924).

52. James Dobson, *When God Doesn't Make Sense* (Wheaton, Illinois: Tyndale House Publishers, Inc., 1993), 161.

53. L. M. Montgomery, *Anne of Green Gables* (New York: Bantam Books, 1935), 301.

54. Scott Brown and Sam Carchidi, *Miracle in the Making* (Chicago: Triumph Books, 2001)

55. Peter Kreeft, *Making Sense Out of Suffering* (Ann Arbor, Michigan: Servant Books, 1986).

56. Margery Williams, *Velveteen Rabbit* (Philadelphia: Courage Books, 1997), 12-13.

Chapter 14

57. C. S. Lewis, *Mere Christianity* (New York: Macmillian Publishing Company, 1960), 104.

58. F.J. Sheed, *The Confessions of St. Augustine* (London: Sheed and Ward, 1984).

59. Albrecht Schoenherr, "Dietrich Bonhoeffer: The Message of a Life" (*The Christian Century*, November 27, 1985), 1090-1094.

60. William Wilberforce, *Real Christianity* (Portland: Multnomah Press, 1982), 65.

61. Elisabeth Elliot, *In the Shadow of the Almighty* (New York: Harper, 1958), 15.

62. Peter Kreeft, *Heaven: The Heart's Deepest Longing* (San Francisco: Ignatius Press, 1989).

63. Rick Warren, *The Purpose Driven Life* (Grand Rapids, Michigan: Zondervan, 2002), 42.

64. C. S. Lewis, *The Weight of Glory* (San Francisco: HarperCollins, 2001), 26-27.

65. Ravi Zacharias, *Recapture the Wonder* (Nashville: Integrity Publishers, 2003), 129.